Screenwriting:
Step by Step

Screenwriting:
Step by Step

User-friendly basic training
for people who dream of
writing for movies and television

Wendy Jane Henson, M.A.

PEARSON

Boston • New York • San Francisco
Mexico City • Montreal • Toronto • London • Madrid • Munich • Paris
Hong Kong • Singapore • Tokyo • Cape Town • Sydney

Series Editor: Molly Taylor
Editorial Assistant: Michael Kish
Senior Marketing Manager: Mandee Eckersley
Editorial-Production Administrator: Annette Joseph
Text Designer and Electronic Composition: Carol Somberg
Composition Buyer: Linda Cox
Manufacturing Buyer: JoAnne Sweeney
Cover Designer: Joel Gendron

For related titles and support materials, visit our online catalog at www.ablongman.com.

Between the time website information is gathered and then published, it is not unusual for some sites to have closed. Also, the transcription of URLs can result in typographical errors. The publisher would appreciate notification where these errors occur so that they may be corrected in subsequent editions.

ISBN 0-205-41829-5

Printed in the United States of America

10 9 8 7 6 5 4 3 2   VHP-IA   09 08 07 06 05

Contents

Screenwriting: The FIRST Six Steps

Screenwriting: The **NEXT** Six Steps

Screenwriting:
Step by Step

Screenwriting: The FIRST Six Steps

Introduction:
LEARNING TO WRITE DRAMA

In 1933, Richard Boleslavsky, a brilliant director and acting instructor, published an insightful little book called *Acting: The First Six Lessons.* Three decades later when I was training to become an actor, I treasured that book. I identified with "the Creature," as Boleslavsky calls the young woman who comes to him for lessons. Years later when I began to direct plays and teach young people, I often returned to Boleslavsky's pages, remembering what it is like to have great desire but little skill. Because actors do on the stage what writers do at their desks, much of Boleslavsky's acting instruction also applies to writing drama.

I began to invent stories for my dolls when I was 2. I tackled a first novel at 11. (Much to my mother's surprise.) My first published story ran nationally just after I turned 15. But my dream was always to write plays. After college, however, playwriting went on hold. I did drama. Acted. Designed sets. Painted them. Did lights. Stitched costumes. Dabbled with makeup. Taught in public schools. Produced and directed plays in school gymnasiums as well as in nice theaters with a full array of theatrical equipment. All the time, I was writing articles, stories, and poems. But plays eluded me. (Looking back, I think I simply wasn't ready.)

When at last I began, my experience with theater and writing made me think the transition from narrative prose to playwriting would be simple. On the contrary, it was incredibly difficult. Literature and drama are different art forms. Each has its own fundamental requirements. I had to "unlearn" some things about prose writing and relearn dramatic fundamentals so my plays would work.

As painters must understand color, or dancers acquire technique, dramatists need to learn their art so they can create effective material. To that end, they must study the special needs and challenges that dramatic writing presents.

Usually working alone, poets and narrative prose authors focus on the art of writing. As a rule, their goal is publication. Poems and narrative prose use words printed on a page to describe and explain people, places, and things. Typically, when the poem or story appears in print, the writer's task is finished. With drama, however, things change.

Drama is a collaborative art. A dramatist's primary goal is performance. Unlike novelists and poets who are free to write for themselves, we create behavior for other people to perform. The addition of the actor puts writers into a whole new world. More than a different way of thinking, we must develop a different way of seeing and feeling. Our best bet is to step into the actor's skin.

Consider an actor's tools. The first and most important is his brain. The second is his body. Doing a variation on the philosopher René Descartes, "We think before we behave." No, we do not sit and ponder each breath we take and every move we make. Mostly, the process happens at the subconscious level. But some kind of mental activity comes before a physical action. For example, somewhere in the recesses of our gray matter, we decide to stand up and cross the room before we move. Simple, yes? But people who lose their mobility know this basic process becomes very frustrating when the body can't respond.

Regardless of whether we write material for the stage or the screen, words printed on paper are not enough. Indeed, a script is, and must be, a "blueprint" for a production. Typically, an audience will never touch a film script, let alone read it. All they know is what they see and hear from the actors. Because actors work in three dimensions, dramatists must "think and write in three dimensions." Our material must guarantee the actors' mobility and expression. Our lines must be SPEAK-able. The behavior we create must be DO-able. All of it must go together in a manner that makes sense to the people who watch the show. To that end, playwrights need a working knowledge of both literature and drama. Screenwriters add yet another art form: FILM. It's a lot to learn.

In *The First Six Steps*, we begin with the fundamentals that govern drama in our culture. These are nothing new. Aristotle first formulated them in *The Poetics*, and they have been developed and refined for centuries. They are basic concepts that help you understand what makes drama so you can write drama. They are your tools just as a carpenter has his saw, drill, and hammer.

You can learn dramatic fundamentals through trial, error, rejection, pain, and frustration. But that's the long, slow, hard way. I want to give you clear, simple, user-friendly guidelines that can get you writing and growing *now*. Is my approach the only way to write a screenplay? No. There are dozens, many of which conflict. Many of which I studied before I found a method that worked. But, I wondered, why should writers spend months, even years, wading through a sea of information, seeking a method that works?

So I reviewed existing manuals, interviewed other instructors and studied the best screenwriters in the business. In 12 years of my own experience, I've met my share of producers, directors, and agents, all of whom taught me about writing and the business. Selecting the basic elements upon which they tend to agree, I put the information together in a sequence and style that beginners can grasp and I hope they will enjoy. The following reviewers also provided helpful comments: Steven Bidlake, Central Oregon Community College; Eton F. Churchill, Penn State University, Harrisburg; Terry McAteer, Felician College; and Barry Russal, Palm Beach Community College. The results are designed to help you write a script that is technically correct as well as creative.

Some people scoff. Preaching against "how-to" books and study courses, they say learning dramatic fundamentals kills creativity and causes a "cookie-cutter mentality." But why? Every art has its technical requirements. Think of painters. They must secure a new canvas to the frame, stretch it, and prime it. Does that process kill their creativity and give us cookie-cutter paintings? No. Buildings have foundations. Does that give us cookie-cutter architecture? No. Every human being on earth has a skeleton and a spine. Does that make us cookie-cutter people? Of course not.

Learning dramatic fundamentals prepares you for your creative task and offers a foundation—a spine, if you wish—for your material. Then you can add the layers—muscles, flesh, and blood—that will make your script unique.

Chapter 1 Format

Screenplays must be typed and properly formatted.
No one in the industry accepts material any other way.

Screenplay format has evolved during the past century as the visual language that is used to write a story cinematically. Every film industry professional knows screenplay format. While there are some slight variations, if your format is wrong, it's a dead giveaway that you are an amateur. In short, you need to format correctly. Yet improper format is the most common mistake beginners make. Perhaps with serious consequences.

Most agents and producers are too busy to do initial script evaluations. In fact, it's unlikely they will read your script, even when you have permission to submit it. Instead they hire readers who review material and write reports. (In Hollywood lingo, it's called coverage.) Readers earn a fee per script to weed out those that do not meet professional standards. Writers who can't format are automatically substandard. Therefore, many readers glance over the first few pages of your script. If your format passes muster, they begin reading for content. If your format is full of errors, they can give up and toss your script, story ignored, onto the reject pile.

FAIR WARNING! Never give 'em a reason NOT to read your work!

Why the Fuss about Format?

Agents send scripts to producers. Producers send scripts to investors, studios, and TV networks. An agent or a producer might send a script to an A-list actor. If a script is improperly formatted, poorly punctuated, and full of typos or spelling errors, agents and producers can't show it to anyone. Or *they* will look like amateurs. For them to avoid such scripts saves time, trouble, and embarrassment.

Why Format First?

According to David Trottier, author of *The Screenwriter's Bible,* "Formatting is more than a bunch of rules. Imagine writing poetry in iambic pentameter, but not learning about iambic pentameter until the last minute. That format is part of the poetry. I think where new writers miss the boat is they see formatting as mere rules for margins and tabs that they must use to present their story. They don't see how formatting should be part of the story itself."

Another person said screenplay format is the container in which you put your ideas. Like a crystal vase full of roses, format makes your ideas stand up so your story stands out.

YOUR FIRST DRAFT

Be advised that established screenwriters can get writing assignments with a synopsis or a treatment. Novices rarely do. (If ever.) Writing narrative prose descriptions does not prove you can deliver a screenplay. The industry wants to see a completed *spec script.* (Spec is short for *speculation.* You write a script and speculate that you can sell it.)

Always follow film industry standards for a first draft. Never follow a final draft, a director's draft, or a shooting script, all of which you can find on the Internet. Such scripts have format details that do not belong in a first draft. (PLEASE NOTE: Industry people will call your script a first draft until a producer commissions a rewrite. Also, because "new" and "fresh" are buzzwords in Hollywood, a script that's been around for ages can get a cool reception. Just keep mum about how many revisions you have done.)

Don't Worry! Be Happy!

Standard screenplay format can be annoying, but it's not the bug-a-boo some novices make of it. The good news is that less is more. Good format is clear, clean, and simple. If you write with a computer, know your word processing program so you set up your document correctly at the start. Some people still use typewriters. If you do, you must tab frequently and remember to limit your dialogue to a column 3.25 inches wide.

In the Appendix, there is a Layout Grid template that shows current industry placement of margins and tabs. There are also sample script pages. Let these items be your guide.

Once you have set up your margins and tabs, do a page in screenplay format. Be careful to include correct line spacing and punctuation. Compare your printed text to the grid and to the sample script pages. If your work matches, or at least comes really close, your setup is good. Otherwise, make adjustments.

Don't obsess. The idea is to have a neat, clean, professional-looking page. Being a bit off—let's say an eighth of an inch—is not a deal breaker. But if your action paragraphs are double spaced, and your dialogue column is 5 inches wide, you've got a problem.

START WITH THE CORRECT FONT

Courier is the industry standard font. With an old computer printer or a typewriter, use Courier 10 CPI. If you have a newer computer printer and Windows, a common font such as Courier New 12 is fine. On the Internet, you can download free fonts such as Hewlett Packard's Dark Courier that work well, too. Under any circumstances . . .

REMEMBER! ALWAYS use Courier. NEVER vary the font size.

Don't let the font numbers confuse you. In the early days of computer printers, people measured fonts by width. CPI means characters per inch. (The higher the number, the more characters per inch and the smaller the type.) Now, True Type fonts are determined by height and measured in points. (The higher the number, the bigger the type.)

Courier New 12 means the letters are 12 points high, but Courier New 12 still has 10 characters per inch. Therefore, Courier New 12 *equals* Courier 10 CPI. Dark Courier 12 and all True Type Courier 12 fonts will measure pretty much the same. Check the following examples. When in doubt, grab your ruler and measure.

RIGHT: `This is Courier 10 CPI.`

WRONG: `This is Courier 12 CPI. (Too small!)`

RIGHT: `This is Courier New 12. (10 CPI)`

WRONG: `This is Courier New 10. (Too small!)`

Again you may be wondering, why is the industry so picky? In the days before changeable typewriter elements and computer printers, there were few fonts to worry about. The most common was Courier 10 CPI. Producers found that in a script typed with Courier 10 CPI, a page of text equaled one minute of playing time on the screen. A 120 page script would run close to the industry ideal of two hours. This knowledge also helped readers to time placement of dramatic elements such as plot points. Now, of course, we have a wealth of fonts, but they can vary greatly in width and height. Therefore, different fonts can put different amounts of text on a page.

RIGHT: `This is Courier New 12. (10 CPI)`

WRONG: This is Times New Roman 12. (15 CPI)

WRONG: **This is Verdana 12. (13 CPI)**

See what I mean? All fonts are not created equal. Without Courier 10 CPI as a standard requirement, a 120-page script can run shorter or longer than two hours, and dramatic structure becomes hard to predict. That's why industry people want Courier 10 CPI. Indeed, a producer once told me, "There are ways I'll bend, but when it comes to Courier, I put my foot down."

To Get Clear, Sharp Text

Use fresh, clean, white paper. Choose at least 20 lb. bond. Erasable paper smudges, so avoid it. Also avoid onion skin or colored paper. If your computer printer has a tractor feed, use bond that leaves clean, sharp edges when you remove the feed strips.

With a computer printer, make sure you have a new cartridge so your text won't fade in the middle of a run. With some printers, however, Courier New 12 prints light and can make your text hard to read. Some software lets you darken Courier New, but if yours won't, simply write your script in bold face. Of course, using bold can widen lines. If you "select text" and add bold after you finish the script, you must check and perhaps reformat the entire thing. Therefore, if you use bold, do so from the start.

With a typewriter, make sure you have a good print element and a fresh, new ribbon. Carbon gives clearer, sharper results than nylon.

Setting Your Margins

Producers are rigid about margins for the same reason they are rigid about fonts. Standard margins give a standard page count and a good approximation of playing time on the screen. If scripts run too long or too short, some beginning writers think changing the margins will fool readers. But readers have a practiced eye, and a ruler can quickly determine if margins are correct. (Never cheat. You *will* get caught.)

LEFT MARGIN: 1.5 inches minimum; 2 inches maximum

RIGHT MARGIN: 1 inch minimum. Never less. Also, never right justify. Leave the right edge of your text jagged. (It makes your script easier to read.)

TOP MARGIN: 1 inch

BOTTOM MARGIN: Between 1.5 and 0.5 inches. This can and will vary, depending on your dialogue and action paragraph breaks. One inch is preferred, however. Stay as close to it as possible. Never use less than 0.5 inch.

Things to Leave Out

The following can make a script difficult to read or a film hard to plan. Therefore, industry pros banished these things from spec scripts. Do *not* use them.

1. Scene numbers

Numbering scenes is the director's job, depending on how he wants to shoot a film. If a writer puts them in, the director has to cross them out and renumber, wasting his time and energy. (If you find scene numbers on a script by a name writer, ignore them. Perhaps it was not a spec script, or it is an old script, or the writer was also a director.)

2. CONTINUED at the top and bottom of each script page

Long ago, when computers first became screenwriting tools, printers couldn't be trusted to put CONTINUED where it belongs. The convention became a headache. Since the industry has enough headaches, the detail was dropped. Now screenwriting software does the job. But now, too, producers want shorter scripts. CONTINUED serves no purpose in a spec script. It adds bulk without content, so we leave it out.

 # SCREENWRITING SOFTWARE

Screenplay format is a basic, professional skill. Screenwriters need to know it. Period. It should come to you as easily as breathing. You should be able to set up a page and start writing without a second thought. You simply can't take for granted that you will always have special software available to do the job.

Moreover, computer software is only as good as its operator. Intended primarily for professionals, screenwriting software contains features they need but unproduced writers should avoid. This can lead to mistakes.

For my first class assignment, my students write several pages in screenplay format. Invariably, I must return papers that were done with script software. The papers have scene numbers, CONTINUED at the top and bottom of each page, and transitions such as CUT TO at the end of every scene. These are things that the software has put on the page. Not yet sure what belongs in a spec script, my students figure if it's in the software it must be right. Or else they didn't know how to disable these undesirable elements.

Finally, screenwriting software is expensive. Most beginners are experimenting. As they learn the realities, many decide screenwriting is not for them. Why spend a chunk of money for software before you're sure you want to be a screenwriter? Even for the determined, few first scripts sell. So screenwriting software represents a substantial investment the student isn't likely to recover in the near future.

In fact, no beginning screenwriter has to pay for software. People with basic computer skills can find templates on the Internet that work well and are absolutely free. For instance, you can download Screenstyler, an MS Word compatible template at http://www.screen2screen.com. I use it and have for years. When you use Screenstyler, remember that it is a *template*. Save it to your MS Office files as a template (with the .dot extension). Open it as a template. Whenever you close your script file, save it as a template. Otherwise you may lose the macros.

LAUNCHING YOUR TEXT

Between the Lines

Proper spacing is crucial:

SINGLE SPACE = NO blank spaces between lines

DOUBLE SPACE = ONE blank space between lines

TRIPLE SPACE = TWO blank spaces between lines

Follow instructions exactly for line spacing between screenplay elements such as action paragraphs and dialogue. Always compare your pages to the sample pages in the Appendix. If your pages look considerably different, you have work to do.

Your Title Page

Your title page identifies you and your script, so make it neat and correct. Again, follow the example in the Appendix. Begin with your title in CAPS, underlined and centered, about 3 inches down from the top edge of your paper. *In the lower right corner*, in single space, type your name, address, city, state, zip code, and telephone number. Use a simple block format, leaving 1-inch margins from the right and bottom edges of your paper.

Never put your name on any other script page. Avoid WGA registration numbers and other ownership marks. (Plastering ownership everywhere indicates you're an amateur.)

Writing Page 1

See the sample in the Appendix. Never put your name on page 1.

YOUR SCREENPLAY TITLE: An older convention puts the script title on page 1. A more current practice is to omit it. Either is okay. If you use the older method, type your title 1 inch from the top of your paper, in CAPS, underlined, and centered.

PAGE NUMBERS: Begin on page 2, in the upper-right corner of the page. Put them in Courier to match your text. Numbering pages is essential, so remember this step.

BEGINNING YOUR TEXT: After your title, double space down. At the left margin, in CAPS, type

FADE IN:

Note the colon, and please remember to use one. At the end of your script, type

FADE OUT

Note there is no colon. And please remember *not* to use one.

Use of FADE IN and FADE OUT is another older screenwriting convention. Now, some industry people say the terms are redundant. (Hollywood hates anything redundant.) If you delete these terms, no one will care. But if you use them, make sure you do so correctly. FADE IN and FADE OUT appear only once: at the very beginning and the very end of your screenplay. Never use them anywhere else. After FADE IN: —if you use it—double space down and begin your first scene.

The Scene Heading

Flush with your left margin, type your first scene heading. Also called a *slug line*, a scene heading is basically a scene's title. It is short, simple, and typed in CAPS. It begins by giving the scene's *general* location: INT. for interior or EXT. for exterior. Then the heading specifies an exact location, such as LIVING ROOM, STREET, or SUPERMARKET. It shows that your scene takes place during the DAY or at NIGHT.

EXT. DISNEY WORLD - DAY

INT. AIRPORT - NIGHT

Note the above format, especially its spacing and punctuation. Always use this basic pattern. Always keep the same spacing and punctuation.

WARNING! Use all technical terms correctly and avoid redundancy. For example, EXT. means exterior, and INT. means interior. Yet beginners often write:

```
EXT. OUTSIDE THE PALACE

INT. INSIDE THE COTTAGE
```

If you were an industry reader, and you saw such scene headings, what would you think of the writer? Of course, the lines should read:

```
EXT. PALACE

INT. COTTAGE
```

ALSO! Keep scene headings simple and uncluttered. Never jam them with details such as

```
EXT. A HEAVILY TRAVELED STREET NEXT TO AN APARTMENT
BUILDING WHERE SUE LIVES - 10 A.M. ON MAY 5, 1992
```

Save details for the action paragraph which will follow your slug line:

```
EXT. STREET - DAY

May 5, 1992. Morning. A busy street. An apartment complex.
```

Writing the Action Paragraph

Sometimes the action paragraph is called "descriptive" or "narrative." I prefer the term *action paragraph* because I want my students to avoid description or narration. (Indeed, Aristotle said drama should be "in the form of action, not of narrative.")

Screenwriters use action paragraphs to give brief, clear, simple statements of unspoken story elements that they want the audience to see. In fact, in a screenplay an action paragraph should be so brief and simple that it's more like a list than a description. Single space *within* action paragraphs. Double space *between* them. For content, present the "given circumstances" of your scene. That means:

- The setting. (A busy shopping mall. A quiet garden.)
- Aspects of the environment that can influence a character's behavior. (Time. Season. Weather.)
- Physical details that provide unspoken clues about the characters and the story. (A special prop such as a framed photograph. A dozen roses. A magic potion.)

Above all, however, action paragraphs include your characters' stage business. This is nonverbal behavior that demonstrates personalities and emotions. For instance:

```
INT. LIVING ROOM - DAY

Barbara moves among the plants with a pitcher of water.
Crooning and making libations.
```

Setting the Scene

Details about your story's environment usually come first. There's no rule about how to present them, but beginning with time, season, and/or weather can quickly convey the mood you seek. The location and its important physical features can follow.

```
EXT. PARADE GROUNDS - DAY

Early morning. Blue sky. Bright sun. Heat waves shimmer
above the grass. Bleachers line the field. Red, white, and
blue bunting drapes a reviewing stand.
```

PLEASE NOTE! Screenplay description amounts to bare essentials. In the above paragraph, you get just enough information to realize it's early on a hot day and there will be a military ceremony. Such minimal description is an industry standard and a producer preference. Yes, screenplays go through a series of readings, but don't let that confuse you. Producers give their readers specific guidelines to follow. From one filmmaker to another, those guidelines fit drama. Readers seek scripts that they know will work as drama on the screen. They aren't looking for short stories or novels.

True, you want to engage the people who read your work, but if you describe a sunset with Venus sparkling on the horizon, you're barking up the wrong tree. Film people hate that stuff, and the phrase "Your script reads like a novel" is a complaint. Some industry readers even say that they skip action paragraphs and read only the dialogue. I once heard a director grumble, "I don't need all that single-space crap. Just tell me where the shot takes place, who's in it, and what they do."

But, you ask, how does a writer convey mood, meaning, and human behavior without description? The key is to work for these things:

- Visualize the scene. (See it in your mind.)
- Decide what circumstances and behavior you want the audience to see.
- Write visual images that convey meaning without explanation.
- Write *only* details a camera can capture and/or actors can perform.

In our parade ground scene, the details are brief, but a camera can photograph them. Without explanation or narrative, the visual images can cause certain expectations. For example, morning light looks different from afternoon or evening light. Although it's morning, we see heat waves shimmer above the grass. That indicates the season is summer. The parade ground setting suggests a military ceremony. The bunting colors indicate the country is the USA. In the United States, what patriotic summer holiday rates a military ceremony? Memorial Day? The Fourth of July? What kind of behavior might we expect from characters who appear in such a setting? Now, for the sake of discussion, let's try a rewrite.

```
EXT. PARADE GROUNDS - DAY

Morning. Lead gray skies. Snow covers the grass. Bleachers
line the field. Red, white, and blue bunting drapes a
reviewing stand.
```

Only one element changes: the weather. Summer has turned to winter. The first scene hints at Independence Day. We think of parades and picnics. The second scene hints at Veterans Day in cold gray November. This puts a visual chill on the story. Logically, the audience will expect Fourth of July characters to behave differently from those who are observing Veterans Day. By changing just one image, we can change the entire story.

Camera Angles and Editing Instructions

Terms such as ESTABLISHING SHOT, CU (close up shot), POV (point of view shot), CUT TO, and DISSOLVE are not strictly taboo. But novice screenwriters do well to avoid them. Let the director decide how to shoot and edit your film.

Likewise, avoid phrases such as "The camera finds and goes with . . ." Indeed, never mention the camera at all. I strongly suggest that you cut "we see . . ." or "we hear . . ." The editorial "we" went out of favor years ago. Using it won't get you killed, but it makes your work look dated. That's poor psychology for film scripts.

If you see a produced script that has camera angles and editing instructions, *ignore them.* The industry tells us to leave these things out of spec scripts. Again, why waste time doing things the industry wants us to avoid? The mark of a good screenwriter is to handle text in a way that implies camera angles and editing without "calling the shots."

- EXT. PARADE GROUND (Implies a wide angle shot.)
- Bunting drapes a reviewing stand. (Suggests a medium shot.)
- Lt. Darren Guy steps to the microphone. (Could be a closeup.)

As for transitions, the end of every scene is automatically CUT TO unless the writer states otherwise. So using CUT TO at the end of every scene is like CONTINUED at the top and bottom of each page. Unnecessary. Redundant. Adds bulk without content.

BEAR IN MIND! When you submit a screenplay, you're applying for a job. Your script is your application. Producers are your prospective employers. They want you to meet their requirements for a spec script. They prefer that you leave technical jargon out of your spec script, so it's wise to heed that request. Producers don't care if your scene ends with a SMASH CUT. But they do care whether your story works as drama on the screen.

Introducing Characters

In action paragraphs, when you introduce your characters for the *first time,* put their names in CAPS. Afterward, use normal upper and lower case letters. For example:

```
EXT. PARADE GROUNDS - DAY

Early morning. Blue sky. Bright sun. Heat waves shimmer
above the grass. Bleachers line the field. Red, white, and
blue bunting drapes a reviewing stand.

LT. DARREN GUY, in dress uniform, appears at the podium.
Tapping the microphone, Darren listens to see if it is on.
```

From the start, give important characters proper names. "A woman talks a man out of a suicide attempt" is vague. "Jane persuades Ed not to jump" gives your characters life. It makes them more real and helps you set their action. On the other hand, you can introduce "extras" or background characters with generic names: TWO POLICE OFFICERS, A WAITER, or A CROWD. You put them in CAPS, also. Afterward they, too, revert to normal upper and lower case letters:

```
EXT. PARADE GROUNDS - DAY

PEOPLE take their seats in the reviewing stand. Some of the
people carry flags. A COLOR GUARD marches onto the field.
The color guard has its flags unfurled.
```

A Deadly Question

A student once asked, "Should I treat a dead body as a character?" My answer was, "Only if it speaks." Sometimes before you introduce characters, you have to make sure they qualify as characters. In drama, characters participate in dramatic action. If your dead body starts off as someone with spoken lines and behavior, treat it as a character. Give it a name. Introduce it with CAPS in an action paragraph. If your DB just sprawls, inert, it belongs to your given circumstances. Part of the set. Kind of like a prop.

Writing Dialogue

Dialogue begins 3 inches from the left edge of your page. Confine it to a column 3.25 inches wide. (Never more than 3.5 inches.) From the left margin, indent 2.7 inches, or from the left dialogue line, indent twelve (12) spaces. Type the speaking character's name in CAPS. Single space between the character name and the spoken lines. As follows:

```
                LT. GUY
          Good afternoon, ladies and
          gentlemen. Please rise for our
          national anthem.
```

Things to Avoid

Like margins, dialogue width affects the length of your script. Dialogue that is too wide or too narrow can add or delete pages, thereby throwing off your structure.

Also, it's considered bad form to split dialogue between pages, especially without proper format. For example:

```
                MARCIA
          It's been a long day. I'll rest
          and start fresh tomorrow. It
          wears on me. This turmoil. I
```

```
                    wonder how I will manage.
```

You see? The lines simply stop at the bottom of one page and begin at the top of the next page, giving no clue about who is speaking. NEVER break dialogue this way! In fact, try not to break dialogue at all.

Film dialogue tends to be terse. If your speeches often spill from one page over to the next, you may be into the "Hamlet Syndrome." Writing soliloquies. Your characters tend to think aloud, reciting thoughts, feelings, and facts. Such speeches kill action. If your dialogue often runs more than 5-6 lines, you need to ask why.

There are ways to rewrite so you don't split your dialogue between pages. For example, you can add a bit of business to interrupt the speech:

```
                    MARCIA
          It's been a long day. I'll rest
          and start fresh tomorrow.
```

```
Going to the bar, she pours a brandy.
```

PAGE BREAK==

```
                    MARCIA
          It wears on me. This turmoil. I
          wonder how I will manage.
```

Another option is to have a second character interrupt the first character's speech, even if the second character says only a word or two.

```
                    MARCIA
          It's been a long day. I'll rest
          and start fresh tomorrow.
```

```
                    JOHN
          Good idea.
```

PAGE BREAK==

```
                    MARCIA
          It wears on me. This turmoil. I
          wonder how I will manage.
```

PLEASE NOTE!   When resuming an interrupted speech, some sources put CON'T or CONTINUED beside the speaking character's name. That's another old convention you really don't need. Simply treat the resumed dialogue like it's a brand new speech, as I did in the example above.

Most of the time, these simple devices do the trick. Occasionally, of course, some lines defy adjustment. If you truly can't avoid splitting a speech, the correct format follows:

```
                    MARCIA
          It's been a long day. I'll rest
          and start fresh tomorrow. It
                    (MORE)
```

```
                    MARCIA (CON'T)
        wears on me, this turmoil. I
        wonder how I will manage.
```

IMPORTANT!   Following a split, have at least two (2) lines of dialogue on each page. Never leave one line dangling. Some writers use the full word CONTINUED, but CON'T is fine. Finally, some scriptwriting software automatically puts in MORE and CONTINUED, but be careful. The bias against splitting dialogue is so strong that it's best to disable that aspect of your software.

SPECIAL CIRCUMSTANCES

Parentheticals

These "stage directions" for speaking characters are a word or two typed in parentheses, single spaced between character name and dialogue. (Never use more than three words in a parenthetical.) They reveal behavior that is not obvious from reading the text. They begin 2.2 inches from the left margin or six (6) spaces from the left dialogue line. Limit them to a column 1.5 inches wide.

```
                    LT. GUY
                  (singing)
        Oh, say can you see...
```

An Ongoing Debate

Many industry pros consider parentheticals, like camera angles, an intrusion. They say, "Leave acting to actors, and directing to directors." Moreover, they claim, when a script is properly written, parentheticals aren't needed. To illustrate:

```
EXT. SHIP YARD - DAY

A harbor. A replica of a pirate ship lies at anchor.
DEMONSTRATORS walk with picket signs.

                    DEMONSTRATORS
                  (laughing)
        Down with the Jolly Roger! Down
        with the devil ship!
```

We expect demonstrators to be angry, but my parenthetical says they are laughing. So I can argue that my stage direction gives an unexpected interpretation to the scene. Yet many film folk will balk at this simple usage. Because, they will point out, I can introduce the characters in my action paragraph as LAUGHING DEMONSTRATORS. Then I can delete the parenthetical.

Well. Okay. They're right. We rarely need parentheticals. In fact, with novice screenwriters, they tend to become a crutch and a plague. Why? Beginners are insecure. They feel compelled to explain things. They use parentheticals so readers will "get" the story. Soon, unfortunately, every speech has a parenthetical attached.

No! STOP! When you use parentheticals, you're directing on paper! Success with screenplays depends on writing strong visual images and dramatic action. If you fear people might misunderstand your scene, rewrite it. Redo your images and action until your meaning becomes clear without giving sidebar instructions. When you truly need parentheticals, limit them to verbs that *express behavior.* Always avoid adjectives or adverbs that describe behavior. For example:

```
(smiling)    instead of  (cheerful)  or  (cheerfully)
(tensing)    instead of  (nervous)   or  (nervously)
(seething)   instead of  (angry)     or  (angrily)
```

Remember that you write for professional interpretive artists. If you have done your job, your given circumstances and the tone of your dialogue will give directors and actors adequate clues. Ninety-nine percent of the time, they can play the scene without further input from you.

Scene Changes

Beginners often puzzle over when and how to change a scene. Here's a good guideline: A scene is dramatic action that happens in one place, at one time, with one purpose and one set of characters. The following parameters may indicate that a new scene is due:

Changing location and/or time. (ALWAYS)

Adding or subtracting characters. (OFTEN)

Changing a scene's dramatic purpose. (SOMETIMES)

Gradually, you will develop an instinct for these changes. Just remember that a new heading (slug line) signals a scene change. Again, line spacing is crucial. When you change scenes, double space between the last line of your current scene and the heading of your new one:

```
EXT. SHIP YARD - DAY

A harbor. A replica of a pirate ship lies at anchor.
Laughing DEMONSTRATORS walk with picket signs.

                    DEMONSTRATORS
          Down with the Jolly Roger! Down
          with the devil ship!

EXT. BEACH - NIGHT

Sunset tarnishes the Atlantic. On a windblown beach, SANDRA
watches TIM, her teenage son, scramble along the rocky
shore.
```

See how that works? Type the last line of your current scene. Insert one (1) blank space. Type your new scene heading. You may see scripts that use triple spacing—two (2) blank spaces—between scenes. My sources say between scenes, either double or triple spacing is okay. Just be careful. Never use triple spacing at any other time.

Sound Effects

When your characters and/or the audience hear a special noise, you will need to write a sound effect. Sound effects will appear only in action paragraphs. Always type them in CAPS. Use only a word or two that names the SOUND. That little visual cue is all you need to show a sound effect is desired. (Never use SFX nor list sound effects in a separate column.)

How can you tell what is a sound effect and what isn't? One guideline is to look for the source of the sound. Can you see what makes it? If not, you should write a sound effect. For example:

```
EXT. STREET CORNER - NIGHT

Pouring rain. Lightning and THUNDER. An empty phone booth.
A car passes. The PHONE RINGS. A wandering dog looks at the
phone booth and barks.
```

You can see pouring rain, so you don't need a sound effect. But you can't see THUNDER. So, for the thunder, you must write a sound effect. Likewise, you can see the telephone, but you can't see it ring. You need a sound effect when the PHONE RINGS. You can see the dog, so when it barks, no sound effect is required. On the other hand:

```
EXT. STREET CORNER - NIGHT

Pouring rain. Lightning and THUNDER. A phone booth. A car
passes. The PHONE RINGS. Somewhere a DOG BARKS.
```

Now the dog is *off screen* and *invisible*, so you write his BARK as a sound effect.

TELEPHONES, DOORBELLS, AND RADIOS ARE ALWAYS SOUND EFFECTS. Even if you see a phone or doorbell, you can't see it make sounds. With TV sets, you see the picture. You expect the sounds and know where they came from. But you can't see a radio playing.

```
INT. KITCHEN - DAY

The radio plays SOFT MUSIC. Then there's a BEEP.

                    ANNOUNCER (OS)
          This is a test of the Emergency
          Broadcast Network.
```

Note that (OS) follows the announcer's name. The abbreviation (OS) stands for OFF SCREEN. It refers to spoken lines from an unseen source. Sadly, some beginners get confused and add (OS) to sound effects. No! That's redundant. Simply type your desired sound with CAPS in your action paragraph. You need (OS) only for speeches that happen off screen.

Likewise, use (VO) correctly. This abbreviation stands for VOICE OVER. (VO) is narration that the audience hears, but the characters in the scene do not. For example, on *Magnum P.I.* in the midst of a car chase when Magnum intones, "I know what you're thinking."

Screenwriters use (VO) for exposition. Unfortunately, like parentheticals, it can become a crutch. I strongly urge you to avoid it. But if you can't help yourself, please limit its use to material that is not otherwise seen or heard in the script. Properly formatted, (VO) also follows the character's name:

```
                    MAGNUM (VO)
          I know what you're thinking.
```

Special Effects

Never say how the effects should be done. Hollywood is teeming with technicians who can deliver the look you want. Simply write what you want the audience to see:

```
EXT. FARM HOUSE - NIGHT

A huge silver disk hovers above the yard, HUMMING. An
opening appears. A beam of light descends. Multi-color
ripples within the light become LITTLE GREEN MEN.
```

BREAKING THE MOLD

Some elements found in conventional writing don't belong in scripts. Here are a few:

Passive Voice

I shudder when anybody (especially myself) uses this dreadful verb form. For example:

```
John is being carried by Paul.
```

Passive voice is just plain bad writing, but in screenplays, it becomes a curse. You want to create credible behavior and natural conversations. Passive voice, however, sounds forced and artificial. It makes action hard to read and dialogue clunky. Worse, it opens a door for dangling modifiers that can humiliate you. Imagine your ingenue chirping:

```
                    INGENUE
          Look! A fountain pen lost by
          someone that's half full of ink.
```

Activate! Put your subject at the beginning of the sentence where it belongs:

```
Paul carries John.
```

When the word *by* appears in your script, check your sentence structure. If you have innocently stumbled into passive voice, rewrite.

> INGENUE
> Look! Someone lost a fountain
> pen. It's half full of ink.

Too Many Words

Write lean and mean. Keep action paragraphs short. Cut the details that you can't photograph. For example, "She stands there, thinking." A photograph can't reveal that someone is thinking. Thinking is internal action. So are feeling and remembering. Internal action belongs in books. In drama, if the audience can't see or hear a detail, it doesn't exist. Therefore, you should write only behavior that actors can perform and the camera can capture.

Adjectives and Adverbs

These words describe and explain a character's behavior. You want to show your characters behaving. Description and explanation are the novelist's tools. Your tools are dramatic action and visual images. Ruthlessly cutting adjectives and adverbs forces you to show your characters doing something rather than explaining how they do it. A few descriptive words are okay, but keep them to a bare minimum.

EXERCISE 1

1. From one of your favorite novels, choose a 7 to 10 page excerpt that involves at least two (2) characters and has some dialogue. Prepare a proper title page and write a 3 to 5 page script in standard screenplay format, based on the excerpt from your novel. Use only action (speech and behavior). Avoid parentheticals. Do not use (OS), (VO), nor any other narrative device. (Note: You can expect to cut most of the text.)

2. Watch a favorite movie on video tape or DVD. Then write the first 5 minutes of the script. That is, try to put what you see on the screen into standard screenplay format.

Chapter 2 Character

Typically, when we think of characters, most of us mean the people who populate a play. But there's much more to consider.

Formulating a theory of drama that has been our guideline for 2500 years, Aristotle says we imitate action. Then he says, "The objects of imitation are men in action." (Yes, that means people in action. The ancient Greeks were rabid chauvinists. Don't let Aristotle's culture get in your way.)

It is no wonder, therefore, that in the early 20th century, Konstantin S. Stanislavski, the father of modern acting, equated action with human behavior. Indeed, if action is not human behavior, what do actors imitate? If dramatists write imitations of actions, but we do not create human behavior, what do we create?

Things, such as rocks, trees, and sky, do not have actions. Unless an actor can become stone, sprout leaves, or turn blue, it is impossible to imitate things. Yes, we can imitate grazing cows and scratching chickens, but their actions rarely make for great moments on the stage or screen.

In short, characters are people. Human beings. Regardless of the medium for which plays are written, they focus on conflicts between people. Human beings. Not penguins and not Mack trucks. (Rest assured, if you imitate a penguin having a conflict with a Mack truck, the action will be brief.)

Before you point to films like *Babe, Jungle Book,* and *Toy Story,* remember that the animals and toys have human personalities. The screenwriters portrayed them as people, and Disney regularly proves that we can personify anything. But in drama, a character must display behavior that an actor can imitate. And an actor has to play the part. Failing either of those things, you do not have a character. You can have something else, but it won't be a character.

For Aristotle, the complete concept of character deals with human qualities as well as the choices that people make or avoid. In concert, Stanislavski urged us to understand the psychology underlying the behavior that people display. Let's say you write about a centerfold model who has 27 cats but no boyfriend. Accurate character portrayal will reveal why she is a centerfold, plus why she has 27 cats but no boyfriend.

Indeed, "Why?" is perhaps the most important question screenwriters ask. This is followed by: "Are your characters doing something because it suits them and their situation? Or because it's what YOU want them to do?" Learning the difference is crucial. Never trade something that truly suits a character for something that simply pleases you.

THE DISORDERING EVENT

In drama, when the story opens, a dilemma or crisis occurs that disrupts the characters' lives. It causes a problem the protagonist must solve. Some sources call this the *precipitating* or *inciting incident.* Alternate definitions exist for those terms, however, which can confuse beginners. In his book *On Directing Film,* David Mamet uses the term *disordering event.* To my knowledge, no conflicting definition exists. It stands alone. Clear and precise.

Sometimes a disordering event happens, and then the characters appear. For example, a volcano blows. Next, the audience sees characters scrambling for their lives. This approach is fine, especially in action films where producers need a "big bang" on page 1.

Sometimes we have the reverse. Characters appear. Then the disordering event strikes. For instance, scientists see signs that a volcano will blow. They set out to warn the local residents. Either way, your disordering event is your *point of attack*, the place in your story where dramatic action truly begins.

In his book *Play Directing: Analysis, Communication and Style,* Francis Hodge says of dramatic action, "Whenever two people meet in a play, as in real life, they start 'doing' to each other, and this is what we watch through a time frame." In other words, dramatic action is people *doing to each other.* When your disordering event disrupts your characters' lives, it motivates them, giving them a reason for doing to each other. Solving the problem of the play will end the disruption and restore order. It gives your characters, especially the protagonist, a goal to work for. In the pursuit of that goal, experiences make them grow and change. This is *character development.* And it always begins with your disordering event.

Yes, of course, you can have special, interesting characters in mind before you choose a disordering event. Indiana Jones. Pocahontas. A dizzy dame looking for Mr. Right. A sly con artist. The possibilities are endless. But characters by themselves are like statues. All you can do is describe them. In fact, they become interesting through their behavior. Especially in the way they handle conflict.

In *Gangs of New York,* a gang leader kills a boy's father. Riveted, we watch the boy, grown to manhood, seek revenge. What if the camera simply follows a fellow around New York while he looks for a job? Would we watch? Probably not. The most interesting character in the world doesn't amount to much—until something happens.

CREDIBILITY

Writers want, and *need,* the audience to believe. Whether the story is a preposterous comedy or a far-out sci-fi thriller, the audience steps into a world we create. They must believe, at least for awhile, that the characters are real and the events are unfolding while they watch. To achieve that kind of credibility, the best rule is, "Write what you know." Teachers, established writers, and critics nag incessantly on this point. If you are a typical beginner, you might not listen. Perhaps you will have to learn the hard way. But in the words of the patron saint of writers:

Be patient with everyone, but above all with yourself. I mean, do not curse yourself for your imperfections. And always rise up bravely from a fall.

—St Francis de Sales (1567–1622)

CREDIBLE CHARACTERS FOR YOUR STORY

New screenwriters tend to favor characters they think will impress agents and producers. In particular, rather than write about people they know, they often base characters on "types." The battered wife is a good example. After all, her lot is very poignant and dramatic. But you will get favorable results only if your characters ring true.

I see too many scripts that are simply figments of writers' imaginations. They cover strictly what the writers think, not what the writers know. Guys like to write about gangsters, drugs, and life in the mean streets: *Magnum PI* and *Pulp Fiction.* But I have yet to meet a male novice screenwriter who visits the mean streets, let alone lives there. Novice female screenwriters lean toward *General Hospital* or *Not without My Daughter.* But to date, none of my female students has worked in a hospital, let alone felt the anguish of losing a child.

Both genders like the protagonist as a mindless victim, a hooker-with-a-heart-of-gold or a strong, healthy person who is suddenly, tragically disabled. But as dramatic as those characters may seem, what are their lives like? Do you write about such people because you really understand them? Or because you saw somebody like them on the screen?

Everything is grist for the writer's mill, and "copycat" pieces make good learning exercises. But unfortunately, they aren't viable for movie production exactly because the writer is a copycat. You may emulate William Goldman or Ron Bass, but it's unrealistic to think a producer will pay you big bucks for a rehash of their work. No, folks, you need original ideas with realistic characters. But how do you get them?

There are a limited number of basic plots in the human repertoire. (Estimates run from seven to twenty, depending on the source.) Movies have done them all thousands of times. That means you must bring a fresh perspective, a new twist, a profound perception to these oft-told tales. But, you think, I'm an ordinary Joe or Jane. How can I write something exciting or profound based on me and the people I know?

First, all human emotions are the same. The aspects that change are the environment (time, place, purpose, conditions of life) and the degree of intensity. In other words, if you have ever loved anyone, you know how love felt for someone in China 2000 years ago. If you ever felt joy, you know how a surfer feels catching waves off Malibu Beach. If you were ever frightened, angry, and frustrated, you can understand the feelings of someone kidnapped and held for ransom during the Middle Ages. If you want to portray human emotions accurately, look into your own heart. All the feelings are there.

Second, your realm of personal experience is broader than you think. Often it can serve you extremely well if you run it in tandem with your imagination. For example, one of my students worked part-time as a waitress. She asked what experience a waitress could write about. I mentioned some successful films that have waitresses as central characters. Then I asked, "Now what can *you* do with it? What new twist can you give it?"

When she left class that evening, she was annoyed. By the next class, however, she had an idea for a "crime comedy." Seems it's murder when a nasty restaurant manager "accidentally" gets locked in the walk-in freezer. Of course, one wonders about the sublimation going on, but her script was quite credible—not to mention hilarious.

Another student worked as a car salesman. One day while waiting at McDonald's for his Big Mac, he toyed with the idea of somebody robbing McDonald's and taking a used car salesman hostage. Would he help the bandit get an SUV or a sleek sports car? Where would they go? Would he escape? Or would he perhaps become leader of the gang?

See how that works? Yes, you can base characters on yourself and people you know. You can use personal experience as a springboard. If you need to go beyond it, you can do research. Visit a library. Surf the 'net. Information is plentiful and free.

Let's say you're a bookkeeper from Bloomington, Illinois. You want to write about bank robbers. Many police departments have ride along programs, and many cops will gladly share their stories. Also, prosecuting attorneys and public defenders have public relations people you can talk to.

You're a lumberjack from Lewiston, Idaho, and you want to write a story about Australian aborigines. Try the Internet. Odds are, you can contact an Australian anthropologist. Perhaps you can even trade e-mail with an aborigine family.

By all means, use composites. Melding traits from various people in your life can give you fresh, wonderful characters. For example, let's say your mother is obsessively neat. Let's say another person you know ignores neatness but is a compulsive liar. What do you get if you combine the two? A slob who lies about being a neat freak. Or a neat freak who lies. Period. Either way, you can write the character because of your personal experience with real people who have these traits.

THE "MAGIC IF"

We just discussed people having similar emotions. But you also can give your characters your drives, needs, and desires. These aspects of human personality are similar in all people, so your audience can readily identify with them. Indeed, Stanislavski urged actors to immerse themselves in a character's psychology, using a technique that he called, the "Magic If." An actor must think, "If I were this person, and if I were in this situation, what would I do?" The impromptu quiz works just as well for writers. For instance, bearing in mind the psychology I have assigned to my characters, I ask myself, "If I were my protagonist, Irma, whom the villain, Waldo, held prisoner for 23 years, would I push him over a cliff and laugh while he falls to his death?"

What if Irma, as I invented her, is sensitive, caring, and definitely no killer. If I were that kind of woman, and I did push the brute, I couldn't live with myself afterward. True, I shouldn't "wimp out." But neither can I laugh while he bounces off the rocks. That would be "out of character." I need a more appropriate action. The cliché, of course, is to throw him a rope. Thus, I could save his life and give him a colossal guilt trip.

But what if, early in this flick, Irma showed a steely, cold streak, vowing revenge on Waldo. That "foreshadows" another kind of behavior. In that case, acting as Irma, I can push first and deal with my conscience later. Even if the audience disapproves, they will understand. The key is to *maintain the portrayal* that I invent. If I want to change a character's personality traits, then I must write behavior that suits the change.

Next I trade places, becoming the other characters in my plot. I step into their skins. I poll them for their *reactions.* This step is vital because, in drama, reactions carry great potential for conflict. "If I were Waldo, my cruel villain, facing a 500 foot drop, what would I do?" Stand stiff and unyielding? Plead for mercy? Request a last serving of tea and crumpets?

Once more, I must think. What traits did I give my villain? Did I foreshadow any potential for him to change so he no longer poses a threat to Irma? Did I make him a man who would rather die than face punishment for his crime? Again, I must look inward before I decide, creating behavior that suits my character.

Compare two strive-and-succeed films. *Dirty Dancing* has young people standing up for themselves, shaking their booties with confidence and strength. In *Flashdance,* a young person searches for confidence and strength. While a bit overdone, these films are heart-pumping and foot-stomping triumphs. Johnny says, "Nobody puts Baby in a corner!" Blowing her audition, Alex starts over and makes it work the second time. In the audience, we tell ourselves, "Yes! If I were there, that's what I would do!"

Maybe it isn't. In reality, we might weep or develop a migraine. But as we watch the film, we *believe* we would feel and do the same. Because the emotions and behavior we see are appropriate for the characters and their situations.

THE GLORY THAT WAS GREECE

For western European countries and the cultures they fostered, the art of drama began with the ancient Greeks. A conflict between a character called the *protagonist* and another called the *antagonist* was at the heart of Greek plays. It remains so in modern plays and theatrical films.

In modern culture, however, we sometimes misunderstand the Greek words *protagonist* and *antagonist.* We modern folk too often confuse these terms with hero, good guy, starring role, central character, villain, bad guy, and so on. Yet the film *Citizen Kane* offers a protagonist who certainly is not the central character. *Dead Man Walking* has a Roman Catholic nun as the antagonist. And *Hedda Gabler* gives us a protagonist with a streak of pure venom.

In fact, the roles of protagonist and antagonist are not determined by the magnitude of a role nor a character's ethical code. Rather, they relate to a character's function within the plot. If you are going to write effective dramatic material, you need to understand that function and build on it. How do you get a protagonist and an antagonist? This aspect becomes clearer when you know how the ancient Greeks approached drama.

Originally, ancient Greek plays were part of the rituals surrounding the feast of the Greek god Dionysus. These contests offered fame and fortune to participants. Playwrights and actors prepared for months or even years. In the beginning, the plays dealt with disordering events taken from Greek myths. The earliest plays had a kind of "oratorio" format: an actor recited poems while a chorus chanted commentary. At first, the actors "took turns" performing, much like oratorio and opera singers do today.

Literally translated, the Greek word *protagonist* means "the first actor." In the early contests, apparently this fellow got the coveted role of "opening the show." As Greek drama developed, however, the playwright Aeschylus added a second character—the antagonist—to the stage.

The word *antagonist* comes from *anti-* ("against") plus *agonizesthai* ("to contend for a prize"). At the start, was the antagonist simply the second performer on the bill? We may never know. But the antagonist definitely became the actor against whom the protagonist contended for his prize.

According to Artistotle, "Aeschylus first introduced a second actor. He diminished the importance of the Chorus and assigned the leading part to the dialogue." In other words, instead of having actors address the audience, Aeschylus got them talking to each other. By "inventing" dialogue, he gave us our most basic form of dramatic action. He put the protagonist "in charge," leading the action. The antagonist received and responded. As the characters interacted through speech, more kinds of "doing" developed. The protagonist became leader of the action, and the antagonist became leader of the opposition.

A Game of Chess

There's a lot we will never know about Greek drama, but it's fun to speculate. It seems reasonable that the competition between Greek actors influenced their drama. Perhaps it contributed to the central conflict we see today. Then, as now, competitions and awards carried a lot of weight. Then, as now, winning probably kept an actor working. Certainly the protagonist, as leader of the action, had the best shot at "stardom." The antagonist was kind of a "second banana," since he could only receive and respond. No doubt the antagonist worked harder to get the judges' attention. But I'm sure the protagonist did not sit idle, waiting to be upstaged. And I'll bet both of them hounded the playwright for better lines.

Under any circumstances, regardless of the medium for which we write them, the basic parameters of drama mean that stage and screenplays need

1. At least two characters
2. Dialogue
3. Dramatic action that moves the story forward through conflict

Finding the Protagonist and Antagonist

No matter how many characters populate your plot, the central conflict between the protagonist and the antagonist is the springboard that launches dramatic action for them all. Yet "the protagonist/antagonist thang" invariably confuses new screenwriters.

To make the concept easier, think about a game of chess. The object is to capture your opponent's king. The white king and his forces attack. The black king and his forces respond. The entire game centers on a conflict between these two kings. What happens if you take away one king? Then you have no game. In drama, it's the same thing. Without a protagonist and antagonist, you have no play. (You may have something else—a documentary or a dramatic reading—but it won't be a play.)

How do you distinguish between the protagonist and the antagonist? It's easy when their behavior clearly defines them. The story has a good guy and a bad guy. Light and dark. But a well written script has many layers, and the best characters come in shades of gray.

Consider *The Godfather.* Michael Corleone wants to be free from his father's gangster existence. Michael is a good man. An honest man. A war hero. He loves his family. He is fiercely loyal to them. Yet his very love and loyalty draw him into the life he wants to avoid. That's good writing. It fits the Greek model of the hero with a tragic flaw. In the course of the film Michael does everything a protagonist must do:

1. Faces the problem of the play and decides to solve it
2. Forces other characters to respond, especially the antagonist
3. Ultimately solves the problem of the play and restores order

For Michael Corleone, these actions are painful and the outcome is agonizing. In the end, he does not get what he wants. (Good resolutions don't automatically equate with happy endings. Indeed, they can be heartrending.)

Primarily, the protagonist wants something, and the antagonist somehow keeps him from getting it. A prince seeking his princess has an evil queen bar his path. A heterosexual man falls in love only to discover the object of his affection is actually another man. A secretary devises a smart business strategy, but her boss takes the credit.

To find the protagonist, begin with the disordering event. Identify the problem it causes. Then look for the character who takes charge and decides to solve the problem of the play. Solving the problem may be exactly what the protagonist wants. (Eloise learns the Zoning Commission plans to close her child-care center.) Or solving the problem may help the protagonist get what he wants. (Catching a bandit gets the Sheriff re-elected.) Either way, the protagonist owns the problem of the play and must solve it.

Meanwhile, the antagonist receives the protagonist's action and resists, thereby frustrating the protagonist's efforts. When you look for the antagonist, avoid confusing the dramatic term with the word *antagonistic,* meaning argumentative, hostile, or belligerent. In drama, the antagonist can be those things, but it isn't necessary. In fact, the antagonist can be loving, subtle, passive, or even unwilling.

For instance, little Annie wants to play in the street. Mommy stops her. Protagonist. Antagonist. Annie wants to do something. Mommy receives Annie's action and resists. Because Mommy is hostile? No. Because Mommy wants to keep Annie safe. The antagonist's behavior is *opposition.* Simply opposing another person doesn't have to mean one is hostile or belligerent toward them.

Consider *Romeo and Juliet.* Romeo, the protagonist, wants to marry Juliet. She receives his love and responds. But because their families are feuding, he killed her cousin, Tybalt. That means Juliet must resist Romeo's desire simply because she is a Capulet. No matter how much Juliet loves Romeo, she is on the opposite side, and she can't give him what he wants. That means Juliet is his antagonist. In the end, Romeo forms a plan that he thinks will bring him and Juliet together. Although the plan has a tragic outcome, it does end the feud, thereby restoring order to the families' lives.

Again, the key is to look for function, not morality nor magnitude of role. In the film *Dead Man Walking,* the protagonist is a murderer, sentenced to death. He sends a letter to a nun, who is actually the film's central character. She receives his action (the letter) and responds (going to visit him). He wants to live. But because he is guilty, she can't stop his execution. The nun is his antagonist simply because she doesn't have the power to give the convict what he wants. In the end, she does give him the gift of love. She brings about changes in him that touch us all. To reiterate, the antagonist is the primary character who

1. Receives the protagonist's action.
2. Leads the opposition.
3. Frustrates the protagonist's effort to solve the problem of the play.

Certainly, if you wish, you can use a traditional view of the protagonist as hero or the antagonist as villain. It is undoubtedly the most "normal" approach to writing dramatic material. But, by all means, avoid locking yourself into stereotypes. Human nature is a mass of emotions, desires, and vagaries. Resistance and opposition happen all the time. When other people frustrate our goals, they aren't necessarily bad nor are they the enemy. They're just people who see things differently than we do.

The next time you join a group activity, look for people who want to do their own thing instead of following the leader. Or consider husbands and wives. How many couples live together with no trace of adversity? Indeed, marriage offers conflict enough for any play, and some fine works have been written about marital struggles. So, when you write for the antagonist, think beyond "bad guy" or "villain." Consider their humanity. Include the desires, needs, and wants that motivate them. Your story will benefit.

Additional Characters

Aristotle tells us that Sophocles added a third character to the action on stage—which really got the ball rolling. Greek playwrights had producers, just as we do. (The money guys have been around forever.) All producers know cutting cast reduces budget. Forgive me, but I have this image of a Greek playwright watching a rehearsal while his producer mutters, "We got two actors talking while ten more explain everything they say. What's up with that? Lose the chorus. Give their lines to one actor. Think of the money we'll save."

Of course, I'm being facetious. Over the centuries, however, the Greek chorus faded. Individual characters took its place. Siding with or against the protagonist. But, rest assured, having more characters doesn't alter the common thread of the central conflict.

PUTTING MY FOOT IN IT

Borrowing from George Bernard Shaw, some film folks say the only rule is that there are no rules. So what I'm about to say is dangerous. But I must take a stand. Students often ask if they can have multiple protagonists or antagonists. I say no! Not in drama!

By definition, the protagonist leads the action. The antagonist leads the opposition. How many leaders can you have before they cancel each other out? We don't have multiple protagonists and antagonists for the same reason we don't have multiple presidents of the United States. Or multiple popes. Or multiple queens of England. Multiple leaders defuse power and confuse issues. Their people can't decide whom they should follow. So they fight. The same thing will happen in your screenplay.

Consider a lottery. If several contestants win, they split the money. Likewise, multiple protagonists or antagonists split the action. To visualize the effect, think of watching several TV sets, each running a different story. You can't focus. You get lost. You stop watching. So will your audience.

Often my beginning students claim, "This film has two protagonists" Or, they say, "This one has no antagonist." In fact, these observations are optical illusions. They happen because, quite simply, the students keep confusing protagonist with "hero" and antagonist with "villain."

Some movies have no negative characters. In such cases, you may find the protagonist easily. Naming the antagonist, however, can throw you a curve if you look for a "bad guy." Instead, seek the true parameters for protagonist and antagonist. Consider this example:

When Harry Met Sally

THE DISORDERING EVENT *When Harry met Sally. (Yes, folks, that's it. Plain as the nose on your face.)*

THE PROBLEM OF THE PLAY *Harry fears marriage will ruin their friendship.*

HOW DOES THE PROTAGONIST TAKE CHARGE OF THE PROBLEM? *He dates Sally (for ages).*

HOW DOES THE PROTAGONIST SOLVE THE PROBLEM? *Harry decides to marry Sally.*

In this film, the characters are nice people. There really are no "bad guys." But no antagonist? Rubbish. Throughout the film, Sally receives Harry's action. She wants him to marry her. She opposes his fears. Still, the decision to marry Sally must come from him. He owns the problem of the play. He leads the action. She responds and resists. Protagonist. Antagonist.

A HELPFUL HINT Typically with a "relationship" film, such as a romantic comedy, the two characters in the relationship will be the protagonist and the antagonist. After you identify the problem of the play, simply decide which character owns it and which character frustrates the efforts to solve it.

Subplots also cause confusion. Often they intertwine tightly with the central plot. Story lines blur. Then it seems as if there are multiple protagonists and antagonists. A subplot, however, is less well developed, and its resolution will not solve the problem of the play.

Conditions and Critters

Students often ask if they can have a non-human protagonist or antagonist—such as Nature or the bear from *The Edge.* My answer is, "No! Not in drama!"

Go back to the Greeks. Remember that we imitate men (people) in action. Remember that the words protagonist and antagonist meant *actors* who portrayed *characters.* Characters reveal conflict through human behavior, such as dialogue. How can "things" like Nature fill those requirements?

What if Nature becomes your protagonist? Nature has no actions that an actor can imitate. (How does one imitate a blizzard or an earthquake?) It has no emotions. It doesn't think. It can't take charge of a problem and decide to solve it. How will you write dialogue for Nature? What will Nature say? And who will you get to play the part? No. Unless we personify Nature, it can't be the protagonist.

On the flip side, what about Nature as the antagonist? In *Cast Away,* a plane crash strands Tom Hanks on an island. He struggles against Nature to survive. Therefore, Nature must be the antagonist. Right?

Again, drama is *the imitation of human action.* What human actions does Nature have that an actor can imitate? And who will play the part? Also, the antagonist is the actor against whom the protagonist contends for a prize. The antagonist receives the protagonist's action and responds. How can Nature accomplish those things? No. Unless we personify Nature, it can't be the antagonist.

In that case, who is the antagonist? To find out, we must identify the disordering event and the problem of the play. In fact, a man stranded on a desert island is not the disordering event. It's the first act turning point. To identify the element we need, we must go to the beginning of *Cast Away.*

Chuck Noland, a UPS employee, wants to go home to his sweetheart, Kelly. When his plane crashes and he gets stranded, he fights to survive. Why? Because he loves Kelly. He wants to be with her. She frustrates him simply because she isn't there. She is his antagonist. Indeed, the central question of this film is, "Will Chuck return to Kelly?"

Then, you say, does Chuck not struggle against Nature? Of course he does. But that struggle is not the protagonist-antagonist conflict. It's the problem of the play. It is the condition of life that he must survive so he can return to Kelly.

What about Wilson? Okay. Throughout most of the film, the protagonist is alone. It is very hard to sustain audience interest with one actor talking to himself on the screen. For sure, Chuck needs a sidekick. (Pardon the pun.)

When a volleyball washes ashore, Chuck paints a face on the ball and treats it like another character. This is risky. With a lesser actor, it would be absurd. But thanks to his enormous talent, Hanks personifies Wilson and gives him life. This is a rare event. To sell a script that has such a device, you need an actor like Tom Hanks to back you up.

At this point in the discussion, my students like to hit me with the JAWS shark. It's a living creature, so it has emotions. And it can think. Certainly it receives action and responds. Yes, but how many lines did the shark get? And who played the part?

Okay. If the shark can't be the antagonist, who is? Let's give *Jaws* some thought.

Begin with the disordering event. A shark attacks people at a popular beach. A scientist recognizes the problem and decides to solve it. That decision makes our scientist the protagonist. He urges the local authorities to close the beach. (A sensible plan indeed.)

What character—a role an actor plays—receives the protagonist's action and resists? The town mayor. He resists closing the beach because it will scare away tourists. (Strangely, he doesn't worry what blood and guts in the water will do for them.) The mayor is the antagonist.

Now wait. Before you start throwing things, think. The scientist wants to close the beach. What if the mayor says, "Absolutely. We'll do it right away."

End of film. *Finis.*

The scientist still might decide to hunt the shark, but the mayor's cooperation removes the threat to human lives. This, in turn, takes away a dire need for the scientist to do anything. Eliminate the conflict between those two men and you stop the film. In its tracks. The mayor's refusal, however, forces the scientist to do more. It sends him in search of the shark. Because if he does not go, more people will die. Catching the shark becomes his goal. He takes greater risks because he wants to restore order to his world.

The protagonist and the antagonist are—and must be—*characters whom actors can portray.* (Or at the very least, creatures with human personalities for whom actors can do voice-overs.) You can't do drama any other way.

Now. Let's say you're in a really good mood, and you give me the benefit of the doubt. Maybe the shark does not qualify as a character, meaning it can't be the antagonist. But it darn sure has to be *something.*

Yes. Of course. For one thing, the *Jaws* shark is a powerful metaphor, representing the horrors that life can throw at us. But above all, it's the problem of the play. Sometimes, as in JAWS, the problem overshadows the central conflict. Yes, the antagonist can be the problem of the play. But that's not required. The two can operate independently.

Another inquiry I often hear is, "Can one character be both protagonist and antagonist?" Case in point: *Dr. Jekyll and Mr. Hyde.* Taken from Robert Louis Stevenson's novel, the story adapts well to drama. It has had many incarnations for the stage and screen, including a musical and a version entitled *Dr. Jekyll and Ms. Hyde.*

The story does offer an actor a chance to play two roles, but don't let that confuse you. Dr. Jekyll most definitely is the protagonist. Hyde, however, is not the antagonist.

The protagonist leads the action. The antagonist leads the opposition. Can one player do a tennis match? Think of football or basketball. Can the captain of one team lead the other team at the same time? Of course not! Then what is Mr. Hyde? He is the dilemma that disrupts Dr. Jekyll's life. Again, the problem of the play. To find Jekyll's antagonist, ask who discovers Jekyll's secret and resists it. Which character tries to stop Hyde's rampage? I vote for Jekyll's lawyer and friend, John Uttington. But in various scripts, the role has gone to others, including women who love Jekyll and want to marry him. Someone other than Jekyll, however, does receive his behavior. Someone else responds and resists. Someone leads the opposition.

A Road Block

People in and out of drama often confuse the problem of the play with the antagonist. If you are one of those people, typically your action stops cold and your story fizzles. If this happens, go to the beginning of your script. Review your disordering event. Find your problem. Find the character who decides to solve it and leads the action. Find the character who leads the opposition. These simple steps should get you back on track.

EXERCISE 2

Rent *Citizen Kane* from your video store and watch it carefully. (No alternative. You must see this film.) Next view at least one film from each column below:

Fly Away Home   *The Emperor's Club*

Best in Show   *O Brother, Where Art Thou?*

The Perfect Storm   *What Dreams May Come*

If you have seen these films, please see them again so they are fresh in your mind. If they aren't among your favorites, indulge me. Jot down the title of each show and write a "laundry list" analysis that includes:

THE DISORDERING EVENT *(A dilemma or crisis that disrupts the characters' lives.)*

THE PROBLEM OF THE PLAY *(The protagonist must take charge and solve it.)*

THE PROTAGONIST *(How does he or she take charge and try to restore order?)*

THE ANTAGONIST *(How does he or she resist and frustrate the protagonist's efforts?)*

THE MANNER BY WHICH THE PROTAGONIST SOLVES THE PROBLEM

Sleepless in Seattle

DISORDERING EVENT: *A woman dies.*

THE PROBLEM THAT ARISES: *Her husband loses emotional connection to their son.*

THE PROTAGONIST: *The boy. Wanting to restore his relationship with his dad, the boy writes a letter to a radio talk show, seeking another companion for his dad.*

THE ANTAGONIST: *The father. He refuses to meet a woman who answers the letter.*

THE MANNER BY WHICH THE PROTAGONIST SOLVES THE PROBLEM: *The boy persuades his father to meet the woman.*

Theme

Characters must touch the viewers. Their actions must generate a sense of recognition, feelings of concern, and a desire for "payoff," an emotional outcome that feels logical to the audience.

Every writer faces the question, "What is your script about?" Once when an agent asked, I launched into, "It's about these people who . . ." He cut me off. "No. Don't give me a biography. Just say what your script is about. You should be able to tell me in a few words. One sentence at the most. If you can't, you don't know what it's about, and your material isn't ready for submission."

It was a humbling moment. But his attitude is typical. As a rule, industry people can't and won't spare time for long explanations. So you better be ready when they pop the question. A strong theme statement can be an important part of your reply.

PREPARING A THEME STATEMENT

Your Subject

Humans are psychologically based creatures. We feel first and behave second, expressing our inner feelings through physical actions. In short, our emotions compel and propel our behavior. Of course, as noted earlier, external influences alter human emotions. Time, place, conditions of life. But drama begins with the emotions themselves. For example, Indiana Jones is a bullwhip-toting archeologist who seeks the Lost Ark. But *Raiders of the Lost Ark* is not merely about an eccentric scientist and a missing treasure. (If it were, it would be a documentary.) In fact, the subject is *triumph*. A good man confronts an evil man. An emotional tug-o-war ensues. The film's lively given circumstances . . . Indy's exotic profession, his urgent quest, the dangerous setting . . . provide a strong frame for the characters. But by themselves, these details won't hold an audience.

We want to share feelings with Indy. Fear. Determination. Excitement. That's why we buy a ticket. Indeed, every film story begins with human emotions. Therefore, the subject of your story needs to be an emotion or a condition that has an emotional connection. You should be able to state it in one word: a noun. For example, you could choose love, hate, courage, or guilt.

At this point, we're laying out the bare bones for your story, so we want to keep things simple. Choose basic feelings that will spark your characters' behavior. Attributes such as values and ethics are layers you can add later. There are no restrictions except the kind of story you want to write. Your subject can be lofty or completely depraved. (Indeed, the Seven Deadly Sins are dramatic fast food for screenwriters.)

Of course, no writer can say everything about love, hate, joy, sorrow, or any other subject within the two hour time limit of the average screenplay. So if you wish, use an adjective to narrow the emotional field. For example, *love* can be mother love, unrequited love, forbidden love, or adulterous love. Be very stingy with your descriptive words. Never use more than two.

Now you have your subject. Jot it down on a piece of paper.

Your Basic Action

The emotion you choose for your subject will motivate your characters, making them do things to each other. Next you can decide what behavior the emotion makes the protagonist display. (His action then prompts the antagonist and other characters to respond.) The best way to express the protagonist's behavior is to choose the *-ing* form of a transitive verb. (A verb that shows behavior going from one character to another.) Write this verb, ending in *-ing*, beside your subject. For example:

SUBJECT	BASIC ACTION
Mother love	Protecting
Courage	Fighting
Loneliness	Searching
Reconciliation	Forgiving

Okay. Now you have a subject and a basic action. Put an "arrow" sign between the words: emotion behavior. The arrow indicates that the emotion *leads to* the action.

SUBJECT		BASIC ACTION
Mother love	→	Protecting
Courage	→	Winning
Loneliness	→	Searching
Reconciliation	→	Forgiving

Each combination launches behavior which can go from one character to another. Opening the door for the other character's reaction. People doing to each other.

IMPORTANT! Choose a basic action (behavior) that links logically with your subject (emotion). For instance, "mother love" leads to "protecting" seems quite logical. Odd combinations, such as "mother love" leads to "killing," may be original ideas, but they also can create a credibility gap that destroys your story. Your play must *make sense* to the audience. If you choose an illogical basic action, you may need incredible skill to create a script your audience will believe.

If you decide to try an odd combination, use your given circumstances to tip the credibility scales. For what logical reason might a loving mother kill her children? If it's 2000 years ago, they're Jewish, and they're trapped at Masada, you have a poignant tale that will make complete sense to an audience.

If your character is like the Greek witch Medea, who killed her sons because she hated her husband, you must motivate her behavior so your audience knows its cause. They won't approve. No doubt they will be outraged. But they need to understand. Even bizarre science fiction tales must be grounded in genuine emotion and logical basic action. If your subject and basic action don't fit properly, try other combinations. Work until you get a logical "mesh."

The Goal Sentence

For the next and final step of constructing your theme statement, you will write your *protagonist's goal.* This short, simple sentence goes under your subject/basic action equation. It states what your protagonist wants to do and names the antagonist who receives the action and resists. The goal sentence must evolve logically from your subject and basic action. Crucial because it sets the focus for your central conflict, this last little element often trips up those writers who confuse the protagonist and antagonist. To keep the characters straight, use the method below exactly as you see it written:

NAME THE PROTAGONIST, THE "DO-ER" OF THE ACTION (Hamlet . . .)

IN A FEW WORDS, STATE WHAT HE WANTS TO DO (Hamlet wants to get even . . .)

NAME THE ANTAGONIST WHO RECEIVES THE ACTION AND RESISTS (Hamlet wants to get even with King Claudius.)

See how that works? How straightforward and simple it is? By all means, keep it that way. You can add details later.

The subject/basic action equation and the goal sentence form a complete theme statement. For example, if the play is *Hamlet:*

justice   →   killing

Hamlet wants to kill King Claudius.

The subject is justice. The basic action is "killing." Hamlet, the protagonist, leads the action. In his quest for justice, Hamlet forces Claudius to respond and resist, setting the focus for the central conflict. (Will Hamlet kill the king?)

If the film is *ET:*

separation → getting help

ET wants a boy to help him go home.

The subject is separation. The basic action is getting help. ET leads the action. His desire to go home forces the boy to respond and resist, simply because the boy doesn't have the power to do what ET wants.

Or *My Fair Lady:*

acceptance → teaching

Prof. Higgins wants to teach Eliza proper speech so society will accept her.

The subject is acceptance. The basic action is teaching. Professor Higgins leads the action. His desire to teach Eliza forces her to respond and resist.

Again, you need a *transitive verb* that can take a direct object. These verbs are the strongest words in our language. They indicate action that passes from one character to another, causing a reaction. Here are some transitive verbs that will serve you well:

to lead (leading)	to seek (seeking)	to bond (bonding)
to escape (escaping)	to win (winning)	to reject (rejecting)
to save (saving)	to fight (fighting)	to forgive (forgiving)

For the acid test, simply remember:

Subject → Basic Action = Reaction

(Emotion leads to behavior that causes a reaction.)

Avoid subject/basic action equations or goal sentences that seem awkward or don't make sense. With beginning writers, it's common to see elements such as:

murder → killing (murder leads to killing)

love → committing (love leads to committing)

Is murder an emotion? Or is it behavior that an emotion can cause? In fact, it is behavior. Indeed, murder and killing are the same thing. Therefore, the equation is wrong because it has two behaviors. Let's try a rewrite.

hate → killing

Now the emotion *hate* motivates the behavior *killing*.

Turning to the second equation given above, love is an emotion, and committing is a transitive verb. But we use committing in the sense of committing an act, such as murder.

Typically we don't think of "committing love." Instead, we relate love to making a commitment. Or perhaps bonding.

> love → bonding

In this example, bonding is a stronger and more logical basic action.

Things to Avoid

Intransitive Verbs

In particular, avoid *to be* and its forms (*is, was, were*). Some other intransitive verbs are *to think,* and *to have.* Even some verbs that seem like action, such as *to laugh,* actually are "one way" words. They represent actions people do *for themselves* rather than *to others.*

> success → being happy

> Eliza wants to be happy.

"Being" is an intransitive verb, and "happy" describes the state of mind Eliza desires. The statement may reveal her inner struggle to readers, but for actors, it is passive and static. For that, she needs to show behavior that can motivate a response:

> love → giving

> Eliza wants to give Henry Higgins her love.

Aha! There you have plenty of potential for action and reaction. Eliza can foist 'er affections on 'enry, and 'e can frow 'em right back in 'er fice!

It's true, however, that some transitive verbs turn behavior back to the person who does them:

> success → learning

> Eliza wants to learn proper speech.

"Learning" is a transitive verb. But Eliza can't learn anybody else anything. It's "one way" behavior that Eliza does for herself. She is the only person who can respond. No one else can get into the act!

THE ACID TEST

To check your theme statement and see if it works, you can ask yourself brief questions such as those shown below in brackets.

> love *[Who shows it? Who feels it?]* → giving *[To whom? For whom?]*

> Eliza wants to give Henry Higgins her love. *[Will the first character's action force a response from the second character?]*

Your answers should jive, and the elements go together in a logical manner.

THE GOOD NEWS

A proper theme statement is simple and clear. If you read theme statements aloud and they are easy to say, the odds are they will work as drama. If you falter, however, if your statement sounds awkward or forced, you have a glitch. Simply do it over. Try a different subject and/or verb. Adjust the goal sentence until it specifies in plain, simple terms what the protagonist wants.

The Value of Theme Statements

A theme statement helps you set up your central conflict because it makes you identify the protagonist's goal before you begin writing. If you travel in a foreign country, wouldn't you obtain a map? Well, your theme statement is your screenplay's map. Use it before you begin your journey.

Now, think . . . what will your protagonist do to get what (s)he wants? What will happen if (s)he succeeds? What will happen if (s)he doesn't? These questions will lead you straight into the reactions of your other characters.

Yes, your theme statement can change. Your interest in the subject may flag, or you may decide another basic action is stronger. You may even write many theme statements for one story. That's fine. Just choose the strongest.

A TEMPLATE FOR THEME STATEMENTS

You know now that the elements of a theme statement look like this:

Subject → **Basic Action**

Goal Sentence

A learning aid follows that can help you get started writing theme statements. With practice it will become second nature, and you will do it in your head.

Finding the Subject

To identify your subject, you need only to say to yourself, "The emotion (desire, need) that

compels _____ is _____."
    (protagonist's name)   *(your subject)*

Remember to use one word: a noun. It can be a plain, straightforward emotion, such as love. Or it can be a need or a desire with an emotional connection, like success.

In *Citizen Kane,* the emotion (desire, need) that compels <u>the reporter</u> is <u>success</u>.

Finding the Basic Action

To identify your basic action, say to yourself, "A need or desire for _____

(your subject)

motives _____ to _____.

(your protagonist)   *(a transitive verb)*

Therefore, the basic action is _____."

(the -ing form of your transitive verb)

A need for <u>survival</u>—so he can keep his job— motivates <u>a reporter</u> to <u>investigate</u> Charles Kane. Therefore, the basic action is <u>investigating</u>.

Finding the Goal Sentence

To write your goal sentence, say to yourself, "_____ wants to

(your protagonist)

_____ in spite of _____

(a few words stating the protagonist's wish or desire)   *(your antagonist)*

who _____."

(a few words stating the antagonist's opposition)

<u>The reporter</u> wants to <u>find the meaning of "rosebud"</u> in spite of <u>Charles Kane</u>, who <u>died without leaving a clue</u>.

Keep Sentences Simple and Avoid Details

"Driven by heartache, Dick persistently strives to win Jane's heart in spite of her engagement to a bumbling Neanderthal football player named Tom."

Such rambling will only confuse you. Delete descriptions. What does the protagonist want? What does the antagonist want? Use plain language and make short, clear statements. "Dick wants to win Jane in spite of her desire to marry someone else."

When you finish with *Citizen Kane,* your theme statement should look like this:

CITIZEN KANE: survival → investigating

The reporter wants to find the meaning of "rosebud" in spite of Charles Kane, who died without leaving a clue.

Remember, always use the above sentence patterns and fill in the blanks. It's okay, however, to discover the elements in whatever order occurs to you Perhaps you can't think of a subject or basic action, but you have a goal sentence in mind. Great! Write your goal sentence first. Generally, the elements that you already have can help you identify other parts of the equation. Frankly, I often write my goal sentence first. Then I figure out the emotion and basic action I'm writing about. But ultimately, I have all three elements written down.

If your first statement doesn't work, try another. Remember the first time you used a hammer? It looked easy. But you got bent nails. Like other tools, a theme statement takes practice. But once you get the hang of it, you can go straight to the heart of a play or film. When you write, your theme statement promotes clear, purposeful work instead of letting you flounder.

EXERCISE 3

1. Look up the following verbs in the dictionary. Which are transitive (take a direct object) and intransitive (no direct object)? Which will force reactions from a second character?

to go	to defeat	to send	to shine	to take
to dream	to cling	to fight	to hide	to lead
to need	to work	to change	to get	to die

2. Try the direct object test.

    To make sure you have a transitive verb, start with the infinitive *(to love)*. Add the objective pronoun *whom* and a question mark. *(To love whom?)* Does the result make sense and open the door for a response? Think what the response might be. Write down what another character might do. For example:

    To change (To change whom?) If you want to change people, they can refuse.

    To challenge (To challenge whom?) If you challenge people, they can fight.

    Intransitive verbs don't take a direct object, so they will never work:

    To die (To die whom?) If you die people, they can _____.

    Turn green? No. You can kill people. But you can't die them. (At least not without a really big vat and scads of boiling water.)

    Some transitive verbs won't work, either, because they become awkward and clunky:

    To sacrifice. (To sacrifice whom?) If you sacrifice people, they can _____.

    Like "committing," *sacrifice* can mean two things: actually sacrificing someone or "making a sacrifice" for them. For this verb to take a direct object and work as drama, you must sacrifice *someone*. Think! What is your true intent?

    To cling (To cling whom?) If you cling people, they can _____.

    If you cling Sue, how will she respond? On the other hand, if you cling *to* her, she can push you away. But cling is a difficult verb. *Hold* means basically the same thing, but it doesn't need a "helper" word to clarify the action. Any time your verb phrase sounds forced or ungrammatical, try a different verb.

3. Choose five subjects that interest you. Create a theme statement for each. Be sure to include all three parts written in the proper format:

> **Subject** → **Basic action**
>
> **Goal sentence**

BE CAREFUL!   This exercise seems easy, but the simplicity is deceptive. It can seriously tax your imagination to come up with five different theme statements.

Chapter 4 Action

Drama is deeply ingrained in the human spirit. Indeed, we aren't sure how it began. Probably at the dawn of history, some mighty hunter, proud of his latest kill, stood before his tribe and demonstrated his achievement.

Humans are not the only creatures who display. Most species show behaviors that signal a desire to mate or have postures that forge bonds and resolve conflicts. But as far as we know, we are the only animals who pretend to be other members of our species and act out stories that connect us with an audience. In fact, our proclivity for "showing off" has developed into one of our highest art forms. Go around the world, go eons back in the human epoch, you will find someone with a story to present while someone else watches and listens. In primitive cultures, drama first emerged as ritual.

Humans create ceremonies to honor important events. We wear special garments and masks or paint, move according to prescribed patterns, carry special implements, and speak special words. Certainly, ancient shamans had methods to instill awe in viewers and control them. Today, anyone who attends a wedding, celebrates the birth of a child, or pays respects at a funeral will experience the drama that human rituals inspire.

As rituals evolved, people committed words and actions to memory so they could reproduce and repeat them. Gradually, simple recitations began to incorporate dialogue and action. Specific roles emerged with participants playing certain parts. At that point, drama was born, and dramatists found themselves in business.

The word *drama* comes from the Greek word *draein*, meaning "to act" or "to do." The advent of writing preserved drama so it could be repeated and dispersed. But please remember, drama is *not* literature. Modern culture often tries to treat it as literature, and, sadly, many beginning writers approach drama as if it were literature. However, drama and literature are different arts with different requirements and purposes. The narrative prose of short stories and novels is storytelling, but . . .

Drama Is Story-DOING

As we noted previously, literary authors write short stories and novels for people to sit and read. But we write plays for performance:

- By actors who portray two (2) or more characters.
- Presenting a story through dramatic action and conflict.
- On a stage. (In film or TV, the screen is the stage.)
- For viewers who assemble to watch the show.

What is the most important aspect of any play? *Emotional connection.* A movie with "universal appeal" will link the characters' experiences to feelings viewers have in their own lives. This aspect makes audiences care about the characters and what happens to them. The best way to achieve such emotional connection is to study human psychology. Our biological clocks, our responses in love, the way we resolve (or don't resolve) our tensions—all aspects of the human psyche offer grist for the writer's mill.

A good dramatist, therefore, is an avid student of human nature. Although formal training isn't required, college courses such as psychology and conflict management can help you. Always, of course, your best bet is to write what you know. Again, you don't have to experience everything firsthand. But you do need to experience the *emotions.*

For the depths, all humans share the same feelings. Love, joy, hate, sorrow, compassion, fear, etc., are common to every person on the planet. The differences are:

- The given circumstances (the environment in which the emotions occur)

- The intensity with which people feel the emotions

- The behaviors that the emotions prompt

Consider *Space Jam.* Michael Jordan wants to win a very special game. So does Demi Moore's Lt. Jordan O'Neil in *G.I. Jane.* It's a big leap from basketball to Navy SEALS training, so the given circumstances of these plots are worlds apart. Yet they share success as a subject and the underlying emotions are the same.

Generally speaking, extraordinary circumstances generate extraordinary emotions. The greater the risk, the higher the stakes and the stronger the feelings. For instance, you may feel challenged sinking baskets with friends in your local gym, but Michael Jordan's *entire career* rides on one wild, crazy game. Maybe you have struggled through your share of tests, but Lt. O'Neil must risk *her very life.*

For all of that, you and those characters have exactly the same emotions. If you ever loved anyone or anything, you know how love feels. If you ever had a nightmare, you have known fear. If you ever were happy about anything, you understand joy. If you ever had a fly buzz around until you got annoyed enough to swat the thing, you have a glimmer of what it's like to kill. Remember your own feelings. Project them onto your characters in the world that you create.

Indeed, you can extend this principle in other directions. How do you feel when you settle down for a nice, long, comfortable snooze, and the telephone rings? That one change in your environment alters your entire frame of mind. Likewise, instead of winning, what if you lose? What if, in *Space Jam,* Michael Jordan loses the game? What if, after going through so much hell, Lt. O'Neil can't make the grade? Now imagine how your characters will feel when you change *their* circumstances. Think about the difference it will make in the actions you write.

Next, think about how other people respond to your feelings. If you gripe when a ringing telephone jars you from a nap, how does your behavior affect your spouse? Or your parents? Or your kids? Or your neighbors? Ask the same kind of question about your characters. If

Michael Jordan misses an important basket and feels disappointed and frustrated, how will Bugs and Daffy feel? If Lt. O'Neil were to break down and cry, what emotions might the Navy SEALS experience?

Emotion   →   Action (Behavior)   →   Reaction

The pattern is always the same for every character in every script. You begin with a feeling (need, wish, desire), express it through action (behavior) and then write how the other characters respond.

UNDERSTANDING DRAMATIC ACTION

Again quoting Francis Hodge, "Dramatic action is the clash of forces in a play—the continuous conflict between characters." He emphasizes that dramatic action happens in the present tense, "The participants . . . are always in a state of 'I do' not 'I did.'" This fact is crucial. Regardless of setting, locale or era, from King Arthur to Captain Kirk, characters do their action now. In front of the audience.

For dramatists, however, the word *action* can be very confusing. Modern English often uses *action* as a synonym for *activity*. But in drama, they mean different things. In drama, *action* means *human behavior*, including the underlying desires, needs, and wants that motivate behavior. *Activity*, on the other hand, is the physical means by which characters *express* their desires, needs, and wants.

When I'm thirsty, I feel something. Thirst is my state of BEing. It makes me want or need a glass of water. It motivates me to DO an activity. I go to the water cooler. However . . .

When I arrive, there's this guy with a .45 automatic who says, "Not at my water cooler, lady!" What I do makes someone else respond. Now we have *dramatic action*.

Not only that, but our forces are clashing. We are in *conflict*. I want water. The guy with the gun won't let me have it. What will I do?

If I simply shake in my shoes, that's an activity. If the guy simply points his gun, that's an activity. It's a stand-off. Passive. Static. To keep dramatic action going, one of us must make a decision that forces the other to respond. What if I say . . .

1. "Oops. Sorry. Could I please have a drink?"

2. "Oops. Sorry." Then I tiptoe away, find a phone and call the cops.

3. "Oops. Sorry." Then I whip out my own .45 and shoot him dead.

One situation, three possible decisions. Each creates potential either to end the conflict or to increase it.

If I forget about my drink of water and walk away—or the guy steps aside and lets me have a drink—the conflict is over. In drama, when the conflict is resolved, the story ends. To keep dramatic action—and my story—going, I must keep the conflict going. For example, with the above scenario, I can draw my little cup of water and throw it into the guy's face. That should rate a response.

Another option is to use one resolved conflict as a springboard for a new one. That certainly will happen if I shoot the fellow. (Because it will put me in conflict with a lot of new characters.)

What your characters do to each other is dramatic action. In their doing, they want different things. That puts them in conflict. The conflict can accelerate. (In drama, it's called *rising tension*.) Or it can end. As the writer, you have a choice.

Activity versus Action

Novice screenwriters often put movement into a script simply because they think the characters should be busy. By now, you know that's a mistake. Every bit of behavior needs to have meaning and purpose. Above all, it has to make sense. Even when the logic underlying an activity is obscure, it must exist.

In *Butch Cassidy and the Sundance Kid,* Sundance surprises the school marm, Etta Place. Points a gun at her. Makes her take her clothes off. We think we're watching an outlaw about to commit rape. Then, as he moves close:

> ETTA
> You know what I wish?

> SUNDANCE
> What?

> ETTA
> Just once you'd be on time.

Now their activities take on a totally different meaning and purpose. But still, their behavior makes sense. The underlying logic exists. William Goldman not only knew what his characters were doing, but *why* they were doing. So should you.

If you don't understand an activity's purpose, neither will your audience. It's just a weed cluttering your dramatic garden.

DOING DRAMATIC ACTION

Okay. You understand dramatic action. It's people doing to each other. A clash of forces. Continuous conflict. Also, you have an inkling of what conflict might be. But in drama, a story moves forward through conflict, so we must deal in depth with that aspect.

Basically, *conflict* is dramatic action without resolution. One character wants something. Another character wants something different. It doesn't have to mean they are yelling, cursing, or beating on each other. (That would be *heated* conflict.) It simply means they have *opposing views*.

Dramatic action is reciprocal. It comes in two parts: action and reaction. One character's doing forces another character to respond. When one character resists another, they are in conflict. For example:

DISORDERING EVENT: My dog escaped and ran your cat up a tree.

You knock on my door. *(half an action)*	I open the door. *(the other half)*
You say my dog is loose. *(half an action)*	I refuse to chase him. *(the other half)*

Taking charge of this travesty, you become the protagonist. You lead the action. (You knock on my door.) I am the antagonist. Your doing forces me respond. (I open the door.) You want me to chase my dog. I refuse. We are in conflict.

If we stop here—if I catch my dog and you go home—we have a resolution. The conflict ends. But what if I slam my door and you call your lawyer?

Each time your doing makes me respond and resist without reaching a "settlement," the conflict grows stronger. This "domino effect" of doing compels the characters and propels the plot.

A REMINDER   As noted previously, conflict doesn't have to be violent. Sometimes it's passive. There is even what I call "negative" conflict. A character does nothing, but his lack of behavior motivates everyone else. (In *While You Were Sleeping,* the antagonist is unconscious much of the time. The fact that he can't do anything starts the other characters doing to each other.)

Translating Thoughts into Deeds

How can you determine the difference between being and doing? If your script leans toward being, how can you switch to doing mode? It's easy! Change verbs.

Take the phrase, "I am sad." These words describe my existence, my state of being. I had an experience that makes me feel sad. I *received* an action, rather than *doing* one. When "I am sad," I sit, silent and static, perhaps waiting for my sorrow to go away. How, then, can other people respond to me?

They can't, unless they're psychic. If I want to engage and involve other people, I must express my sadness physically. I must translate my state of being into a state of doing that others can see. Therefore, I ask myself, "How can I *show* sadness?"

I can cry.

Weeping is physical activity that other people can see. When my son sees my tears, he will do something in return. He might comfort me. Or perhaps he will tease me. But we will have an exchange of behavior. Here are a few more examples:

BE-ing	I am happy.	I am angry.	I am afraid.
DO-ing	I laugh.	I growl.	I tremble.

A character who translates existence into behavior becomes a do-er of action. When you translate being into doing, you become a writer of action. To help you make the transition more easily, use the "Magic-If" and try *role-playing*.

1. Put yourself into a character's place and complete the phrase "I want to . . ."

2. State the action that you (as the character) want to do.

3. Name the second character who will receive the action and can respond.

Sounds like building a theme statement goal sentence, doesn't it? By all means, try to be just that simple and direct.

Let's say your character Jane, a teenage girl, is angry with her brother, John. (Her state of being.) The phrase you give her could be, "I want to punch John's lights out." (Translates being into doing.) John, facing a right cross, has to respond.

The fact that Jane wants to smack John tells us about the kind of person she is. Similarly, John's response to Jane's attack will speak volumes about him. Therefore, you, as the writer, must be careful. You make very crucial decisions about your characters when you choose activities that translate BE-ing into DO-ing.

Let's say John's phrase could be, "I want to duck and escape." Or, "I want to take a swing at my sister." Or perhaps even, "I want to take her in my arms and hold her until she calms down." What will the audience believe about John because of his behavior? This is the *creative* part of screenwriting. Your choices determine the way the audience views your characters, and, subsequently, the direction your story takes. Choose the doing that best suits both.

If John fights back, you will have a very different story than if John takes his sister into his arms and holds her. You must ask yourself, "What do I want the audience to feel? How do I want them to respond?"

Okay. You, as John, say, "I want to duck and run." So John ducks and runs. What's next? Let's jump back into Jane's body. Does she want to scream at John? Or chase him? Or sit and cry?

If you start off well, but your script becomes static and dull, your characters probably have slipped into being rather than doing. With the "I want to . . ." exercise, you can get them back on track and moving forward again.

The Most Crucial Test

Always remember to run a "photography check." A picture really is worth a thousand words, so ask yourself . . . Can I photograph everything in my script?

For example, "She is thinking she should have kept her appointment yesterday." How can you photograph that? I'm sorry. You can't. "His mind is racing." Can you take a picture of a racing mind? No.

Consider the nursery rhyme, "Mary, Mary, quite contrary." Can you tell from looking at a photograph that Mary is contrary? Of course not. Contrariness is a state of being. Mary can look haughty or cross, but a picture alone won't reveal that she's contrary.

ACTIVATE!   Show Mary doing something. Write a scene in which she hires an assassin to murder Elizabeth I. (Now that's contrary!)

Just for Fun

Look at the nursery rhymes that follow. Assume the "creatures" in these verses have human personalities. Do you see dramatic action? If not, can you rewrite to make dramatic action? Use your imagination.

1. Jack and Jill went up the hill,
To fetch a pail of water.
Jack fell down and broke his crown,
And Jill came tumbling after.

2. Twinkle, twinkle little star
How I wonder what you are.
Up above the world so high.
Like a diamond in the sky.

3. Hey, diddle diddle, the cat and the fiddle,
The cow jumped over the moon.
The little dog laughed to see such sport,
And the dish ran away with the spoon.

4. Peas porridge hot,
Peas porridge cold,
Peas porridge in the pot,
Nine days old.

5. Yankee Doodle went to town,
Riding on a pony.
Stuck a feather in his hat,
And called it macaroni.

6. Jack Sprat could eat no fat,
His wife could eat no lean,
And so between them both, you see,
They licked the platter clean.

(*Warning!* This is a trick nursery rhyme!)

ANSWERS: To work as dramatic action, the verbs in these poems first must be put into *present tense*. Next we look for *transitive verbs and their direct objects*. Then we can decide as follows:

1. Yes, there is dramatic action, if we assume that Jack falling down makes Jill fall, too. (The domino effect.)

2. No. There are no characters. To turn this poem into dramatic action, you need one astronaut pointing to the star and another saying, "Oh, wow! Green slave girls of Rigel 12!"

3. Yes. If the critters have human personalities, there's enough dramatic action for a soap opera.

4. No. To turn this pea soup poem into dramatic action would take a miracle.

5. No. Yankee Doodle has plenty of activity, but there's no response from another character. Maybe if the pony could talk . . .

6. Yes. This is an example of "negative" action. What Jack *can't* eat motivates his wife. What she *can't* eat, motivates him. Between them, the pot roast disappears.

STORYTELLING VERSUS STORY-DOING

At an early age, we begin to love the storyteller's art, listening as our parents, teachers, and camp counselors describe intriguing characters and exciting events. We begin to write narrative prose in grade school, using words to explain and describe everything. We acquire a vocabulary of adjectives and adverbs. (Words that describe and explain words.) When we become interested in screenwriting, we hear, "You must be a good storyteller." Thinking we know all about that, we tackle our scripts and submit them eagerly. But they come back with notes that say, "This reads like a novel. Show. Don't tell." We're left to scratch our heads in dismay.

Okay. Here's an illustration:

STORYTELLING: She reaches with her right hand, grasping her opponent's left arm, raising her right leg sharply so her right foot connects with his left upper thigh.

STORY-DOING: She grabs him and kicks him in the groin.

See the difference? Novice dramatists often make their characters describe and explain events when instead the characters should be doing action. To get out of storytelling mode and into story DOING means changing the way we think when we write.

To that end, however, I must steer you through the perilous straits of *backstory*. So, students, raise your right hands and repeat after me, "On my honor, I will do my best to begin with a disordering event." Because a good, strong disordering event is your key to success.

BACKSTORY BLUES

Of course, you need to plan. You need to know more about your characters than their names. That's the point of all your research. There is a difference, however, between providing some background information and writing disordering events that take place off camera before the action begins.

Also called *antecedent action*, these offscreen events stick your characters with the dreadful chore of explaining and describing past experiences and events. They turn into talking heads who dish out facts. Some writers believe this recitation of facts "sets up" a script. No! It kills a script. It's narrative. When narrative begins, action grinds to a halt.

Indeed, you can become so involved with telling the story that you never get around to doing the action. Or you can become such a slave to your backstory that you make your characters behave in unreal or even stupid ways just so your plot will work. In truth, your characters are the plot. They face a crisis. They start doing to each other. Subsequently, the plot evolves from their behavior.

For instance, let's say your protagonist, a rogue astronaut, discovers the moon really is made of green cheese. If earthlings mine it, world hunger will cease. Everybody doubts the astronaut, however, because he is a rogue. There is, of course, an evil government gourmet who wants the cheese for himself.

Okay. You adore this story. You can see your title on the marquee. You can hear Keanu Reeves saying your lines. You plot and plan every detail. At last, you write:

<u>THE CHEESE IS GREEN</u>

FADE IN:

INT. UNITED NATIONS - DAY

The General Assembly is in session. For the past hour, MEMBERS have been listening to a speech made by DASH MASTERFUL, who stands before them, wearing the space suit of a NASA astronaut.

> DASH
> On the moon while I looked for
> rock samples, an astronomical
> discovery was made. A layer of
> green cheese.

A low murmur is heard among the members. AMBASSADOR GOTCLOUT, who has worn a sneer throughout Dash's speech, turns to his ASSISTANT.

> GOTCLOUT
> That Dash Masterful! He's been
> an eccentric rogue since he
> joined the astronaut program.

> ASSISTANT
> General Hoozits will have to be
> called.

To borrow a line from Ace Ventura, "Allrighty, then." This piece begins with backstory—descriptions and explanations of an incident that occurred off screen. Past tense verbs and passive voice rule. ("MEMBERS have been listening to a speech made by DASH MASTERFUL.") Our impression of Dash comes from hearing other characters describe him. (We should draw our own conclusions from watching his behavior.) The characters spoonfeed information to bring the audience "up to speed." The action stops. Cold. Probably the next scene is a flashback—very likely a dream from which Dash wakes screaming—which gives the audience still more information about his past life.

In his book, *On Directing Film,* David Mamet says, "If you find that a point cannot be made without narration, it is virtually certain that the point is unimportant to the story (which is to say the audience); the audience requires not information but *drama.*"

For novelists, the audience sees (and sometimes hears) only words, so a novelist must give the audience information. But this is drama. Instead of being "talking heads" who recite facts, your characters must act and react. Instead of providing information about the past, you must create behavior that propels your characters into conflict. Instead of telling, you must do.

Let's try a green cheese update:

THE CHEESE IS GREEN

```
FADE IN:

EXT. MOON BASE - DAY

The Sea of Tranquility. DASH MASTERFUL, wearing a NASA
space suit, gathers rocks. Sliding one last sample into his
pack, he heads for his Lunar Living Module.

INT. LLM - DAY

Clad in jeans, body tattoos, and a motorcycle jacket, Dash
puts a disk on his CD player. MOZART wafts from the
speakers. Going to his lab table, he dumps his rock
samples. One is pale green. He sniffs. Flips open his
switchblade. And tastes.

                    DASH
          My god! This is cheese!

INT. UNITED NATIONS - DAY

Standing before U.N. MEMBERS, Dash waves a slice of green
cheese.

                    DASH
          We can end world hunger! Achieve
          lasting peace!

The Members murmur among themselves.

AMBASSADOR GOTCLOUT sneers.

Gotclout's assistant taps keys on a cell phone.
```

```
                    ASSISTANT
          General Hoozits? Please hold for
          Ambassador Gotclout.

Gotclout grabs the phone.

                    GOTCLOUT
          Harvey? Dash Masterful just
          finished.
                    (listens)
          Yeah. My office. Ten minutes.
          Bring grenades and bazookas.
```

No, it won't win an Oscar, but at least in this version, the characters do. From his appearance, attire, and taste in music, viewers will conclude that Dash is eccentric. Nobody needs to say so. Transitive verbs in present tense and active voice reveal behavior that makes other characters respond (dramatic action). There are few adjectives and adverbs. (But how many did we need?)

Most important, although the second version is exactly the same story, not one character has to describe or explain anything.

EXERCISE 4

Experimenting with photography can give you huge insights about writing for film. In fact, getting behind a camera is the best and quickest way to understand its effect on dramatic action. This exercise leads you down that all-important path.

If you have a video cam, use it. Or if you have a still camera, try that. As an absolute last resort, you can cut photographs out of a newspaper or magazine.

1. You will need at least 10 different shots (images). Make sure most of them show people doing action. They can be the same people, but the actions must change. (Please do NOT take 10 shots of passing cars, sunsets, and empty rooms.) If you use a video cam, remember a "shot" runs from the time you aim and turn the camera on until you turn it off. If you use a still camera, you will need at least 10 snapshots. Or cut out at least 10 different magazine pictures. You can have a specific plot in mind and find pictures that match. Or you can collect completely unrelated images and "free associate."

2. Run your shots on your VCR or lay your still pictures on a table. Experiment. Try different sequences and combinations. Use your imagination. What story can you think of to go with these shots? Got an idea? Good! Now . . .

    a. Write a sentence that summarizes your disordering event.

    b. Write a complete, proper theme statement.

    c. Write a *silent* movie screenplay, at least four to six pages, based on your shots.

        Make sure to start with a disordering event and follow your theme statement. Have a beginning, a middle, and an end.

        Use at least two characters: a protagonist who leads the action and an antagonist who can receive it and resist. Show dramatic action, but remember . . .

    d. *No dialogue.* Also, you must avoid action paragraph lines, such as "He tells her he is going to the grocery store." (That's cheating!)

FINAL GOAL: Have your characters do a complete story strictly through the use of visual images.

Yes, this assignment is a challenge.

But it's wonderful experience.

And it can be great fun.

Chapter 5 · Structure

Subject, theme, and dramatic action have set your story's focus. Now we must talk about structure—connecting all the basic elements together so your characters can progress logically through your plot.

Taking our cue from Aristotle, we know that every play needs a beginning, a middle, and an end. No, that statement isn't as silly as it seems. Novels, short stories, and essays may have distinct beginnings, middles, and ends. Or they may not. It's not a requirement in narrative prose. But it is required in drama, although in film, the convention can surprise us. According to director Jean-Luc Godard, whose work leans toward avant-garde, every film has a beginning, a middle, and an end. But not necessarily in that order.

For now, however, while you are in the basic learning phase, let's avoid confusion and stick with tradition. (You need to learn the rules before you break them.)

When people watch a play, we need to see the action truly beginning. (The disordering event causes a problem.) At the same time, a hint of what will happen in the middle of the story piques our curiosity. (The protagonist decides to solve the problem, putting him at odds with the antagonist.)

Likewise, in the middle of the plot, clues about how the play will end make us curious about the resolution. Such clues are called *forwards*. Wondering what will happen next literally makes us look forward to the rest of the show.

This "progression of actions" extends the spine of your story. Just as bones hold your physical body together, structure holds your script together and gives you a scaffold upon which you can layer your details. Over the centuries, this "beginning, middle, and end" pattern has evolved into what dramatists call "three-act structure." However . . .

What about a play that has only two acts or as many as five? The mind boggles. How can a two- or five-act play have three-act structure? Because it will have the same three-part principle of beginning, middle, and end. No matter how many "actual" acts exist, the basic concept remains. The way we express the concept simply "moves around."

William Goldman's scripts and his books about the film business are legendary. He is famous for saying, "Screenplays are structure." Yet he also says he doesn't believe in three-act structure. Linda Seger follows the three-act paradigm, but William Froug says it makes scripts dull and boring. This brings the debate around to Goldman's other legendary quote, "Nobody knows anything." No wonder beginners tear their hair!

Personally, I think *three-act structure* is a misnomer. I like *dramatic structure* because it covers the basics that make plots work without nailing writers to some literary cross. It really doesn't matter if a screenplay has three acts or five. The things which the industry says it wants in a spec script are:

- A beginning, a middle, and an end

- A disordering event (the hook or dramatic incident) to start the story

- A central conflict centered on the protagonist and the antagonist

Even for the best dramatists, structure varies. One script may have a strong hook at the beginning of Act One and fall apart at the end. Another may have a shaky midpoint, but it ends with a bang. Creativity, after all, is not an exact science, and human beings are not machines. Nor does striving for good dramatic structure turn us into writing robots. Structure simply gives us a launch pad that helps us gets a script off the ground.

 ## SCREENPLAY LENGTH

In stage plays, there is an intermission between acts. The curtain closes, and the audience leaves the theater for several minutes. Playwrights know they must put a twist or complication at the end of each act that will "hook" the audience and bring them back after intermission, eager to see the rest of the show.

Films, however, have no intermission. Indeed, people leaving the theater are the last thing we want! We need twists and complications in appropriate places that can keep the audience in their seats for the entire two hours. In other words, we omit the intermissions, but we keep the act break "hooks." We call them *turning points* or *plot points*. Where they appear is crucial, and their placement depends on the number of pages in your script.

For years, the industry standard has been 120 pages, about 2 hours of playing time on screen. Currently, there is a trend toward shorter scripts—100 to 110 pages. Still, the act breaks and the related turning points must exist, occurring in the right places at the most appropriate times. In stage plays, it's good to have acts that are similar in playing time so the intermissions can be equally spaced. In film, however, preferences change. The standard convention is to have 25% of the script as Act One, 50% as Act Two, and the last 25% as Act Three. So, a 100 page script would break down like this:

ACT ONE: 25 pages (turning point between pages 20–25)

ACT TWO: 50 pages (turning point between pages 80–85)

ACT THREE: 25 pages (resolution between pages 100–105)

Some people balk at counting pages to determine where important moments such as turning points and the midpoint should occur. But the page count is a guide that helps control pacing so we go steadily forward. (Instead of having moments of excitement that alternate with eons of boredom.)

THE TURNING POINT TANGO

Let's say you write a nice, strong first act. You wonder, "Now what? How do I keep this thing going?" You need a first act turning point. If you write one that turns where it should and goes onto your page with a bang, it will push your characters into Act Two. If not, your story starts to limp. Your characters become like dancers who lose the beat, trying to get back into sync with the music but never quite catching up.

But, gee, what the heck is a turning point? At times in my classes, I have been bewildered, thinking that I already gave a good answer, only to discover I told my students what a turning point does. Not what it *is*. Recently, however, a student blurted out, "Isn't a turning point just another disordering event?"

Bless her heart! Now why didn't I think of that?

Although your first disordering event is the most crucial, your plot can and will have more. Challenges and decisions occur that give your script life. Your first disordering event is your point of attack—your first chance to grab the audience's attention. Strictly speaking, you have 5 to 10 pages to launch this crisis. But most producers will be happy if you put it on page 1.

Your next important disordering event, the Act One turning point, gives the protagonist a new challenge that drives the story into Act Two. It should increase the protagonist's peril while offering new motivation for the antagonist to resist. Your Act Two turning point propels the characters toward the conflict resolution that must happen in Act Three.

Let's look at the film *Contact.* A scientist makes an important discovery but can't pursue it because she loses her research program to budget cuts. Accepting this challenge, she finds enough money to carry on. But at the end of Act One, the antagonist takes credit for the protagonist's success. Again challenged, she competes honestly and fairly with him. He wins through lies and deceit. Things look hopeless. She watches from the sidelines while her rival prepares for the mission she wants. Then at the end of Act Two, a skillfully foreshadowed disaster opens a door so that she can go in his place.

Just as big disordering events cause the most chaos, bold reversals and astonishing twists make the strongest turning points. But giving the audience a jolt may not be necessary. Sometimes turning points are simple, even anticipated. In that case, what your characters do about them becomes your primary source of power.

In *Slingblade,* I sensed where the story was going, and the turning points happened pretty much as I expected. The disordering events did give Karl new challenges, however. Had he shied away, refusing to deal with the events, the story would have died. Instead, Karl faces these moments, making decisions that forever change his life and the lives of the other characters. Far from boring because the story is "predictable," the turning points force Karl to do things that he—and we—wish he could avoid.

In comedies, too, we can anticipate turning points without becoming bored. *Ever After* is an update of *Cinderella.* Watching such a beloved old chestnut, we would be scandalized if the film strayed too far from the basic plot. So the turning points need to happen in the familiar times and places. But the film proves even an oft-told story can have surprises.

Gone is the lovely but timid and victimized girl of the original tale. This Cindy is a fighter with a huge heart, a keen wit, and a sharp sword. And the Prince, although still charming, is something of a rogue. The given circumstances may be the same, but the new characters and their dramatic action hold our interest.

To help you visualize the mechanics of turning points, think of dancing. The music begins. You sway with your sweetheart. Then—amid flashing spotlights—Michael Flatley of *Riverdance* cuts in.

If you are a woman, will you spin away with Michael? Or will you stop him in his prodigious tracks and return to your true love? If you are the man in this disconnected duo, will you pursue your lady and risk getting your toes caught under Michael's machine-gun clogs? Or will you cut in on another couple and steal a new partner?

A decision and commitment are at hand. Or underfoot, depending on your perspective. Whatever choice you make, your life . . . and your dancing . . . will change forever.

A good turning point works the same way.

APPLYING THE PRINCIPLES

In Act One, the first 5 pages are your "beginning" during which:

- Your characters assemble. *(People embark on a hot air balloon voyage above California's wine country.)*

- A disordering event occurs. *(The balloon's pilot has a heart attack.)*

- A problem arises. *(The balloon could crash.)*

During the next 10 pages, you launch your dramatic action when:

- The protagonist decides to solve the problem. *(Marian, a librarian who read a book about hot air balloons, assumes command of the propane burner.)*

- The antagonist receives the action and resists. *(George, an attorney, insists it's illegal for unlicensed female librarians to fly hot air balloons.)*

Next, between page 20 and 25, you write your Act One turning point. Your protagonist faces a new disordering event—a complication or twist—that:

- Turns the characters and the story in a different direction. *(A blast of wind snuffs out the propane flame and blows the balloon out over the Pacific.)*

- Increases the risk the characters face. Especially the protagonist. *(The balloon hurtles downward.)*

- Forces the protagonist into further action. *(Before the tourists become shark bait, Marian spots a desert island and lands the balloon on its beach.)*

Now your characters have a new set of given circumstances to cope with. Meaning your protagonist has an even greater problem to solve. The heat is on!

THE ACT TWO TURNING POINT

Although I don't recommend it, your Act One turning point can be a bit bland. The Act Two turning point, however, precipitates your dramatic climax, the moment of greatest tension in the film. Therefore, your Act Two turning point needs "oomph." Big time. Some Act Two turning points amount to a "moment of truth." The protagonist deals with elements of life (s)he fears or hates to face. Also, "dramatic reversals" are common. In mystery thrillers, for example, the protagonist learns the prime suspect is not the killer. Meanwhile, the REAL killer lurks nearby with a knife.

In another type of Act Two turning point, the protagonist seems defeated. All is lost. (S)he feels helpless. But something goads the protagonist into action. For example, another character is in peril. The protagonist must act quickly to save the innocent victim. Under any circumstances, the Act Two turning point should offer the greatest risk the protagonist has faced so far. Of course, putting one's life on the line is the ultimate peril.

Again, the crucial issue is placement. Yes, some scripts take more time than others to launch. An early or late first act turning point, however, almost always causes problems with Act Two development. With dramatic material, the "domino effect" takes a nasty turn. If one portion of a script is wrong, other parts suffer. Which is why counting those pages can be important. No, you don't have to put your Act One turning point smack on page 20 or 25, but if you haven't written it by page 30, your script could be in trouble.

THE DRAMATIC PREMISE

A good way to be sure your script will have solid dramatic structure is to write a *dramatic premise*. Evolving from the theme statement, the premise is a tool that you can use to state the logical progress of your story in clear, simple terms. While the theme statement shows the human needs, wants, desires, and behavior that motivate your characters, the premise shows how their dramatic action drives your plot. The easy way to write a dramatic premise is to use three simple sentences:

• Line 1 sums up your primary disordering event, the crisis that launches your plot. The goal sentence of your theme statement is a logical and strong foundation for this line.

• Line 2 sums up the Act One turning point, the "hook" that launches Act Two. It sharpens the conflict, builds tension, and propels the characters and story into Act Two.

• Line 3 sums up the Act Two turning point, the "hook" that launches Act Three. It shows the strongest complication the protagonist will face.

By listing your protagonist's greatest challenges and decisions, the premise helps you outline your script. It also keeps reminding you of the problem your protagonist must solve. Linda Seger calls this aspect "raising the central question."

> Hamlet, Prince of Denmark, meeting a spirit who claims to be the ghost of Hamlet's murdered father, hears that his uncle, King Claudius, committed the crime. *(Central Question: Will Hamlet kill the king?)*

> Wanting revenge but not injustice, Hamlet hires players who act out the "murder," making Claudius decide it's time to dispose of the prince. *(Central Question: Will Hamlet kill the king?)*

> Certain Claudius is guilty, Hamlet seeks revenge. *(Central Question: Will Hamlet kill the king?)*

In *Hamlet,* the answer to the central question is yes.

Let's try more examples:

City of Angels:

> Seth, an angel, wants to share life with Maggie. (Will Seth share Maggie's life?)

> Seth reveals himself to Maggie, but when she realizes he is an angel, she rejects him. (Will Seth share Maggie's life?)

> Learning that he can "fall," Seth becomes mortal so he can be with Maggie. (Will Seth share Maggie's life?)

The answer is no.

Scent of a Woman:

> Needing money, a student takes a job as a companion for a blind retired Army officer. (Will the student help the officer face and deal with life?)

> The student goes along with the blind man on a wild fling in the big city. (Will the student help the officer face and deal with life?)

> The wild fling gets the student into trouble at school, forcing the officer to defend the student. (Will the student help the officer face and deal with life?)

The answer is yes.

Sometimes when people do the premise for the first time, its simplicity annoys them. One student remarked, "*Citizen Kane* is about a lot more than the word *rosebud!*" Well, yes. Of course. But we're not writing a blow-by-blow report on creative content. The dramatic premise is a tool. Its purpose is to help you write a plot that is:

CLEAR   **LOGICAL**   **EASY TO FOLLOW**

If you can write your premise easily, your plot most likely has a solid foundation. If you have to struggle—especially if the sentences sound forced or ungrammatical—then something is wrong. Most likely a break in your logic has thrown off the focus. Or perhaps you are pursuing a subplot rather than a central plot.

THE VALUE OF THE PREMISE

Sometimes you have "violations" in logic that stall plot development. The premise can get you back on track. Once you identify the error and return focus to the central conflict, scripts spring to life. The premise applies just as well to the analysis of finished films. Moreover, it comes easily when a plot is strong and bogs down when plots are vague or weak.

Together with your theme statement, the dramatic premise can be a clear, simple outline for your plot. Short and sweet, it is extremely adaptable. If you need changes, you can make them at will, altering only a few sentences rather than several pages. On the bare bones of those few sentences, you can add layers without getting lost. I like to write my theme statement and premise on a sheet of paper. Then I "free associate," jotting down details as I think of them. In the following example, I put some details in brackets:

```
                      THEME STATEMENT:

              love  →  understanding
         Joe wants to understand his wife, Sue.

DISORDERING EVENT: Joe finds his wife, Sue, in bed with
another man.

PROBLEM OF THE PLAY: Joe, a workaholic, loves his wife,
Sue, but never spends time with her.


[When he finds her in bed with another man, Joe demands
that she tell him why. Sue says that Joe doesn't under-
stand her and the romance has gone out of their mar-
riage. She wants a divorce.]


[Joe knows he has neglected Sue. He decides to change.]

THE CENTRAL QUESTION: Will Joe learn to understand Sue
and rekindle their relationship?

Act One TP: Joe "kidnaps" Sue and takes her to a remote
tropical location. [Gilligan's Island. Primitive as can
be. Which Joe thinks is romantic. For Sue, however, who
detests "camping out," it's just more evidence that Joe
doesn't understand her.]

Act Two TP: After days of hearing Sue weep, moan, and
grumble, Joe says the real problem is that SHE doesn't
understand HIM. [Now HE wants a divorce.]
```

The method is fast, easy, and effective. If I toss the sheet and start over, I lose little time and labor. Most important, such a page can become your foundation for a pitch. Agents and producers will ask, "What is your script about?" Of course they mean, "What is the action?" The doing. Frankly, they want your answer in 30 seconds or less. Once you have a theme statement and dramatic premise, you will know how to reply.

EXERCISE 5

1. Write three complete theme statements for three different scripts.

2. For each theme statement write a complete dramatic premise.

Chapter 6

Review and Rewrite

You have inspiration. Then you add perspiration. Almost without fail, 90% of writing is rewrite.

The challenge of finding and cutting or rewriting material that does not belong in screenplays can be perplexing. The literary conventions and tools we have worked hard to acquire suddenly seem out of place. For example, look at the following passage:

```
EXT. COUNTRYSIDE - DAY

It's early summer. The year is 1663 when colonial Dutch
settlers occupied America's Eastern Shore, and mighty New
York City was merely a wooden village called New Amsterdam.
Slipping between green, tree-clad banks past a dark, quiet
farmhouse, the Hudson River shimmers in the pale gleam of
dawn, reflecting a bank of storm clouds that are gathering
overhead. A low rumble of THUNDER breaks the silence.
```

You expect to find such detailed description in a novel. But if you see it in a screenplay, would you . . .

A. Think the script is well written?

B. Object strenuously?

The answer is B. Object. Strenuously. The passage is narrative prose. It reads like a novel. And it includes some elements that can't be photographed. Look at this rewrite:

```
EXT. COUNTRYSIDE - DAY

A summer dawn. The Hudson River. A colonial Dutch farm
house. Clouds boil on the horizon. THUNDER rumbles.
```

CUTTING TO BARE ESSENTIALS

Action is what producers, directors, and actors need. Plus, they tell us, "Write lean and mean." You've learned about writing action. But what is lean and mean? And how do we get our work to turn out that way?

At this point, it's time to read some produced screenplays and see how the pros write lean and mean. But for you to find produced films in screenplay format, they probably will not be published. Screenplays, after all, are "blueprints" for a movie. They aren't supposed to sit on book shelves.

Generally if you do find screenplays published, they will be anthologies (e.g., *Best Films of 1987*). When you find them in books, they will look pretty much the same as stage plays. Okay. Fine. You can read them for content. But nobody could make movies from them. Since getting movies made is your goal, you need to find screenplays in manuscript form.

The fastest and easiest way is to surf the Internet. Sites such as Drew's Script-o-rama (http://www.script-o-rama.com) will let you download anything from first drafts to shooting scripts. In addition, you may be able to find screenplay scripts in your local library, buy them at some of the better bookstores, or order them through catalogs.

When you read produced plays and screenplays, notice how terse they are. Shakespeare is a fine example. (I dare you to read *Hamlet* and find paragraphs that describe and explain the production.) But stage plays allow more description than films ever will.

Drew's Script-o-rama offers the first draft of James Cameron's *Aliens*. Cameron's script has a bit of the novelist's touch. First drafts can be this way to "flesh out" the story. But still, the writing is lean. Action. Dialogue. Visual images. An occasional descriptive sentence, but nothing is wasted on explanations.

Now, take a look at the final draft of *Alien* by Walter Hill and David Giler. This piece is ready for production. Its action paragraphs are truly meager: a few words per line with triple space separation. Yet the story is there. Complete. You can follow the plot with no trouble. Really, however, it's too lean for a spec script, and I don't recommend you write yours that way. But this version of *Alien* clearly demonstrates how few words screenwriters need to put a complete story before the camera. Comparing these two screenplays will give you some idea of how much you can whittle out of your script without losing the story.

GETTING RID OF GOBBLEDYGOOK

The following exercises can help develop your lean and mean skills:

1. For two weeks, force yourself to be simple and concise. Strictly limit every sentence you write to 10 words or less. Eliminate run-on sentences. Break up complex ones. Delete conjunctions *(and, but, also)*. Avoid *as, while,* and all words that create strings of dependent clauses. Cut adjectives and adverbs. (You'll be surprised how few of them you really need.) Build an arsenal of transitive verbs—the action words that convey doing.

2. For one week, watch TV news broadcasts. Notice that the news stories consist of carefully chosen visual and sound bytes. Reporters have only a few moments, so the delivery is "just the facts." Next, thumb through a newspaper or magazine. Find photographs of people doing to each other. Pretend you are Peter Jennings. Report when the events are taking place, where the characters are, who they are, and what they are doing. Practice the exercise until it becomes easy for you for state what you see in clear, simple terms.

3. Poems convey meaning through imagery. Plays—especially screenplays—use visual images. Indeed, drama as we know it began with poetry. In concept, it is closer to poetry than it is to novels. (Poet, novelist, and screenwriter Sherman Alexie thinks of a screenplay as a 120-page sonnet.) Therefore, you can benefit from some of the poet's tools. Study symbolism, simile, and metaphor. Choose a produced screenplay to read, and look for examples of these poetic elements in the script.

4.   Practice phrasing action paragraphs with sentence fragments. (What would happen to Shakespeare, Dylan Thomas, and Dr. Seuss if every sentence required a subject and a verb?) Of course, be careful. Keep your language grammatical, your punctuation correct, and your logic impeccable. Deleting articles *(a, an, the)* or personal pronouns *(his, her, your)* can make your work look like a mental pygmy wrote it, so retain them, by all means. For example:

```
Jerrud ropes the horse. Ties it to a tree. Then approaches,
keeping his hands low.
```

5.   If you have a screenplay written, go through it and eliminate extraneous details. Some early scripts read like Fingerhut catalogs. No action. Just THINGS. Page after page. (It's depressing.) Unless the detail is very important to your plot, don't mention that the hero wears a hand-knit Irish wool sweater. Nor that a living room has Provincial furniture and a southern exposure.

6.   Check your work to see if you are repeating yourself or stating the obvious. Too often, students write the same sentence several different ways. Or use the same words over and over. Or describe something which the character's behavior readily reveals :

```
INT. LAUNDRY ROOM - DAY

Pam who is folding laundry in the laundry room hears the
phone RING and runs to answer it. The phone continues
RINGING. She races down the hall. The phone RINGS several
times more. At last reaching the kitchen, she reaches for
the phone, grabs it, and gasps breathlessly into it.

                         PAM
              Hello? Hello? Hello?

There is no answer. Pam hangs up.

                         PAM
              There was no answer.
```

The above example is painfully bad. And surprisingly common. I know you want everything to be perfectly clear, but saying the same things over and over is a bore. Always cut words you don't need and film people don't want to read. Let's try a rewrite:

```
INT. HOUSE - DAY

The laundry room. Pam folds towels. The phone RINGS. Racing
into the kitchen, Pam grabs the receiver.

                         PAM
              Hello?

DIAL TONE. Pam hangs up.
```

See how that works? Unfortunately, just as some writers balk at screenplay format, many hate being miserly with words. Those who can't or won't understand the need for verbal economy will protest, saying, "But, Ms. Henson, *Squeezing Montana* by Shane Tarentino Coppola is filled with long passages that read like a novel." In particular, students toss *Pulp Fiction* at me as a script that "ignores the rules." To which I reply, "Bunk."

Various drafts of Quentin Tarantino's material, including *Pulp Fiction,* are available on the Internet. Given Hollywood's broad definition of a first draft, these may not be Tarantino's initial efforts. But still, no matter how off-beat his subject matter and his characters, he is a fine dramatist whose scripts are very well crafted. In fact, 98 percent of the "rule breakers" students offer have the correct fundamentals present and accounted for. Students who say otherwise have not read the material or else don't know correct fundamentals well enough to spot them.

Moreover, to any charge that the "big boys" ignore fundamentals, I say, "You're mixing apples and oranges." Most produced screenplays were assignments given to known screenwriters. Those writers have paid their dues. They can sell a script with a pitch. Having established their professionalism, they are pretty much free to do what they wish.

Unproduced novices operate in a totally different sphere. Because they write spec scripts. Producers state clearly what they want to see in a spec script. If you don't like their requirements, you should take it up with them. I think, however, you will find them unsympathetic if you cite established screenwriters who ignore "the rules."

Reality Check

This is a harsh business. Misunderstanding or denial of its requirements can make our lives even more difficult. Our determination to be "different" and not to do what "they" want can complicate our efforts. Because, you see, *they* have the power. Thousands of perfectly good screenwriters will conform to the wishes of producers, directors, and agents. Therefore, it's a buyers' market. They don't need us. We need them. Of course, when you become William Goldman or Ron Bass, you can do what you want. But an unknown, unproduced novice must conform to basic standards.

A novel in screenplay format won't get "their" attention. For your script to have a chance, it has to be drama. Once you nail format, choose a theme, and learn to write action, your next move is to get rid of gobbledygook. Trim out as much as you can.

EXERCISE 6

1. Photocopy at least 5 pages from one of your favorite novels. Take a pen or pencil to the copy and cross out every scrap of narrative prose. Leave *only* the action. (This exercise can be a shocker. You'll see just how much we rely on narrative prose.)

2. Jot down at least 5 simple actions. Then write at least 2 variations. Limit yourself to 10 words or less. For example:

ACTION: Sue puts her arms around John and kisses him.

VARIATIONS: Sue grabs John and plasters him with a kiss.

Sue snuggles close to John and nibbles his lower lip.

Sue sags against John and raises her chin, seeking a kiss.

One kiss, four ways to write it. Simply using different verbs creates different interpretations that an actor will understand.

Be careful! One of my students used the same verb and kept changing adjectives or adverbs. No! That defeats the whole purpose. Do *not* use adjectives or adverbs.

3. Find a produced screenplay to read. Choose one section at least 5 pages long that you feel can stand improvement. Rewrite it.

4. Apply the principles that you have learned in this step in your own Act One. Do your best to make it stronger and tighter.

When you complete this assignment . . .

Congratulations!

You have taken the first six steps.

Screenwriting: The NEXT Six Steps

Introduction:

WRITING DRAMA FOR FILM

In the *first* six steps, we worked on getting basic tools that can help you write drama. These *next* six steps deal with writing drama *cinematically,* expressly for mainstream feature film in the United States. The basic concepts are universal, and this book very well may serve screenwriters in other countries. But spec scripts written for film producers abroad receive somewhat different treatment than they do in the States. For instance, some foreign film industries get government financial subsidies for film and television projects. Therefore, foreign producers might be more willing to experiment, allowing first time writers more latitude than producers will in the States.

In the U.S. market, of course, the system is strictly free enterprise, and commercial success is crucial. One producer took me to task for saying that my script would cost only $3 million to produce, which is a drop in the bucket for Hollywood. "True," he snapped, "but where are *you* going to get $3 million? It's a small budget, but it's still a lot of money."

Trust me. In the United States, the film industry is a business, and the primary goal is making money. Very rarely does a single producer have the wherewithal to write a check for an entire budget. Most producers must find investors who can afford to risk millions with no guarantee that they will get a penny in return. Such people are hard to locate. And they can have some strange ideas about what they want in return for their investment.

Unfortunately, people who can afford to fund films often do not know and do not care about art. More likely, they are business executives who want as much "bang" as possible for their bucks. As a result, they may think more about stars who have box office draw than about the quality of a screenplay. But make no mistake. The producers, director, and actors will think about it. Since nothing succeeds like success, they will cater to the established screenwriter who has experience and credits. Those writers are your competitors. Your only hope of winning this wild and crazy race is to defeat them. You must do what they do as well as—or better—than they do it.

Some prodcos (production companies), such as Disney, generate their projects strictly in house, working only with writers known to them. Others will accept material through agents. But agents are awash with established writers. Most hate to invest the time, money, and energy required to develop a new one. Often the only agents who will deal with novice screenwriters are beginners themselves. They know zip about the industry and have never sold a screenplay. (The blind leading the blind.)

Still, many independent producers are receptive to new writers. *New,* however, does not equate with *raw.* Like doctors, new writers go through a kind of internship and residency, often facing years of hard work for little or no money until they get a break. Indeed, some prodcos have internship programs. If you get into one, you can greatly accelerate the learning process. As always, your best bet is to have original ideas and to write strong scripts.

Therefore, you must become skilled at the craft of screenwriting. It's sad, but true: Very few first scripts sell. Writers can invest time and energy on many projects before they get one that works. It's a good idea to develop a writer's portfolio with at least three scripts, preferably more. Meanwhile, you must learn enough about the film industry so you can find a market. To compete effectively in the market, your scripts need to be a step or two away from production. Always submit material that is finished and represents your very best work.

Yes, lightning strikes happen for some writers. But not as a rule. And certainly not every day. Even for those who stick it out, the rewards are "iffy." The most common scenario is that a producer will option your script for a nominal fee while he or she goes looking for the money to make the film. Therefore, many first contracts state that the writer will be paid on the first day of principal photography. This means, aside from option money, you probably will be paid *only* if and when they start shooting the film. This can take years. Check the development of some famous films, and you will discover that *ET* took 8 years, *Forrest Gump* took 10 years, and *Ghost* took 11. For a film to go from script to screen in 3 years is a walk in the park. So if you hope to make a lot of money quickly, it might be wise to pursue another line of work.

As unpredictable as a crap game, screenwriting has been called a job in which you can make a killing but you can't make a living. A few writers will become millionaires with just one script. For the vast majority, however, a few options or one screenplay sold for a song may be the only return on a lifetime of work. Clearly, screenwriting is no place for dabblers. If you love the craft and can face the challenge, welcome. But, please, friends . . .

Don't give up your day job.

Chapter 1

Act Two

A screenplay takes a protagonist on a journey that changes his life forever. But first the journey must happen in the writer's head.

When you leave your house, you know your destination, right? In fact, it's rather strange for us to leave home without knowing where we are going. Yet, many people launch into writing screenplays without a clue as to where their story will go. They may invest months of work on a trip that meanders through the cinematic countryside. Too often, they get lost. Remember: The disordering event causes a problem your protagonist must solve. As long as you write toward that solution, he or she can work toward it. Therefore, when you begin work, you need some idea of how your plot ends.

Personally, I always know my ending before I start the script. Sometimes I even write the final scenes first. As a rule, however, especially during the development of Act Two, I begin to see other options. Sometimes, these take me on tangents that I am better off without. Sometimes, though, I see that my original ending will not work, and I must choose another. All the while, however, knowing my destination keeps me on track.

WORKING BACKWARDS

When you plan your so-called road map, it can be very helpful to think about your ending and ask, "How did my protagonist arrive here?" Then work backwards. Using *Beauty and the Beast* as an example:

> **ENDING:** The Beast becomes the handsome prince of Belle's dreams. *How does he reach this point?*

> **ACT TWO TURNING POINT:** The Beast sends Belle home, although he knows it may mean his death. *How does he reach this point?*

> **ACT ONE TURNING POINT:** The Beast accepts Belle in her father's place. *How does he reach this point?*

> **DISORDERING EVENT:** The Beast takes Belle's father prisoner.

See how that works? We focus on the outcome. Then we back up a step at a time. Or more appropriately, a decision at a time. The ending is the culmination of all the decisions the protagonist makes. If we can easily follow those decisions back to the beginning of the story, we will have a simple but logical outline of the plot.

A REVIEW BEFORE TWO

ACT ONE: *The Beginning*

1. A disordering event occurs and a problem arises.

2. The protagonist decides to solve the problem.

3. The antagonist resists the protagonist's efforts.

4. The Act One turning point restates the problem and takes the characters in a new direction, driving the story into Act Two.

[25 to 35 pages]

ACT TWO: *The Middle*

1. The protagonist faces new decisions and tries to implement new plans.

2. The antagonist's resistance increases.

3. The protagonist becomes discouraged.

4. The Act Two turning point restates the problem and takes the characters in yet another new direction, driving the story into Act Three for climax and resolution.

[50 to 60 pages]

The development of each act is different. Act One sets up and launches dramatic action; Act Two is where the action becomes intense. Act Two increases risks and forces decisions, constantly sharpening the conflict. Beyond doubt, it is the "workhorse" portion of your script. Notoriously, it's the segment that gives screenwriters the most trouble.

THE DYNAMICS OF ACTION

NEWTON'S THIRD LAW: For every action → there is an equal and opposite ← reaction.

Okay. When you started screenwriting, you didn't plan to study Newton. But just as everything in the universe responds to gravity, you have learned that your characters participate in the push-and-pull that we call dramatic action:

ACTION →

I drop my wallet.

← REACTION

You pick it up.

In our first example in Chapter 4, the initial action was small. (You knock on my door.) The above, too, is simple—even commonplace. Dropping a wallet happens to someone somewhere every day. For people in the audience, both action and reaction will trigger emotions. By far, however, *reaction* has the greatest potential for impact. Indeed, in drama perhaps the best way to express conflict is to write a strong *reaction.* For the novice screenwriter, this is crucial.

Look at the following example:

ACTION →	← REACTION
I drop my wallet.	You pick it up.
I say, "That's my wallet."	You say, "All right."
I reach for it.	You give it back to me.

Simple actions with subdued reactions create a subdued story. On the other hand . . .

ACTION →	← REACTION
I drop my wallet.	You grab it.
I say, "That's my wallet."	You say, "Tough!"
I shout, "Police!"	You run away.

See how that works? My "ordinary" action followed by a strong reaction from you initiates an even stronger response from me. It's the "domino effect." Character reactions intensify conflict and move the plot forward.

Keep 'Em Guessing

Human beings can have fairly predictable responses. If you behave quietly toward me, I tend to have a quiet response. On the other hand, if you scare me, I scream. If you tickle me, I laugh. Yes, if you prick me, I will bleed. When we watch a movie or a play, we expect characters to follow a "normal" behavior pattern. Mostly, they do.

Of course, if we have expectations about characters, and they keep coming true, we begin to anticipate their behavior. In a screenplay, much of the behavior we create is predictable. However, always knowing what a character will do becomes boring. One really effective approach is to write reactions that play against what the audience expects. To give you a few examples:

In *Raiders of the Lost Ark,* Indiana Jones faces a henchman who does a series of wild martial arts moves. We expect Indy to fight. Instead, he simply whips out his revolver and shoots the fellow.

In *Dances with Wolves,* Dunbar, a wounded Union soldier, learns that doctors plan to amputate his shattered leg. It's a tragic situation for him, but not much of a surprise for us. On the other hand, when he drags himself onto a horse and tries to commit suicide by hurling himself at the Confederate forces, our jaws drop.

In *Butch Cassidy and the Sundance Kid,* the title characters find themselves cornered atop a cliff overlooking a river. We expect them to make a stand. Instead, they jump off the cliff into the river—to our delight.

Think. What realistic and logical behavior can you write that your viewers won't expect?

To Stay on Target

Keep in mind everything you did when you wrote Act One!

For weeks, we drill on the first six steps. Many times my students turn in Act One scripts that are so good they bring tears to my eyes. Strong theme statements. A clear protagonist–antagonist conflict. A solid dramatic premise. The tension builds. Their Act One turning point catapults the characters into Act Two, straight as an arrow. ZING! Then I read Act Two. And ker-PLOP! The arrow drops to the ground as if some giant hand strikes it down. What went wrong? I search for clues. Invariably, the writers forgot their original theme statements and lost track of their central conflicts. The worst result? They try to get back on track by reverting to narrative prose.

By now you understand that narrative prose—describing and explaining behavior—tends to kill action. Each time you stop the action to describe and explain it, your story stops in its tracks. To achieve and maintain credible conflict, you need to do the following:

1. Stick with your theme statement, central question, and dramatic premise.

2. Show your protagonist making decisions that your antagonist can resist.

3. Move your story forward through conflict.

4. Show your protagonist taking risks.

These elements should remain constant throughout your script. In Act Two, however, they become crucial. Yes, the game plan for Act Two resembles the plan that you had for Act One. Traditionally, Act Two is twice as long as Act One or Act Three. That makes many novice writers lose their original thread, their "throughline of actions." For me to give you reminders along the way can be very helpful. However, I am not the "plot line police." Once you learn the basic lessons, sticking to your original design becomes your responsibility. It is *every* writer's responsibility.

Fortunately, sticking to plans is a challenge that we learn to meet with time and work. The more you practice, the easier it gets. Here are a couple of suggestions to help you. Post a sign in your work space. On that sign, list your basic elements. Make it a ritual to study the sign each day before you begin writing. Here's an example:

<u>BRINGING IN THE SHEAVES</u>

THEME STATEMENT:
greed = escaping
Con artist Trish wants to escape from her gangster boss.

PROTAG: Trish   *vs.*   ANTAG: Max

CENTRAL QUESTION: Will Trish escape from Max?

DRAMATIC PREMISE:
1. Trish absconds with $1 million that belongs to Max, big time con artist.
2. Disguising herself as a nun, Trish goes to work on an Indian reservation.
3. Life as a nun spurs Trish's conscience and gives her the courage to face Max.

Refer often to Act One as Act Two progresses. Each time you end your Act Two writing sessions, check the emotional tug-o-war between your characters. Does your new Act Two action comply with your original plan? If you have trouble sticking with your original plan, analyze it again. Perhaps it wasn't strong enough. Or while you were writing, you found something better. Change is fine. Just make sure you know what's happening and why.

THE BEAT GOES ON

```
INT. LIVING ROOM - DAY

I hear a KNOCK. I open my front door.

My former college sweetheart stands on the threshold.

                    ME
          Throckmorten! It's been 20 years.

                    HE
          I never stopped thinking of you.

I rush into his arms. He smothers me with kisses. I double
my fist and give him a right cross. He groans.

                    HE
          What was that for?

                    ME
          20 years without a phone call!
```

This brief segment is called a *beat.* Note that it is really a miniature "playlet." It has a beginning, a middle, and an end. It has a protagonist and an antagonist. Above all, it has dramatic action and conflict. In film, it can be done in a single shot.

Stanislavski said that working on a play is like eating a turkey. People who try to swallow an entire bird will choke on it. But if they cut the bird into bits, the banquet can go smoothly. Likewise, if we divide a play into bits, we can master its actions. With his Russian accent, however, "bits" was pronounced "beats." And today "beat" remains with us as the smallest working unit of a play.

Stanislavski's concept applies to writers as well as to actors, and beats are the building blocks for both stage and screen plays. When I asked one of my theater arts professors to define a beat, he said, "It is the beginning to the end of an intention." In other words, a beat begins when a character wants to do something. Either (s)he succeeds or (s)he fails. At that point, the beat ends, and a new one begins. In a good script, each beat will propel the protagonist into more conflict.

RAISING THE STAKES

As you know now, dramatic action develops through a process of a character making decisions and facing the consequences. Such decisions tend to be made under stress. In other words, the protagonist and/or his supporters face pressure from the given circumstances of the story as well as opposition of the antagonist and her supporters. In *The Edge,* a plane crash strands two men—a woman's husband and her lover—in the Alaskan wilderness. They face perils from the rugged setting, the weather, and a marauding bear, as well as from each other. As he should, the protagonist makes plans, hoping that his decisions will resolve the problems. When his plans fail, both men face greater danger. That's what it means to *raise the stakes.*

Think of a poker game. A character has cards he wants to play. (An intention.) He places his bet. (Making a decision.) Meanwhile, other characters have their own cards. (Intentions.) They place their bets. (Making their decisions.) When they have risked everything that they dare, they either call or fold. The first character wins or loses. The hand (beat) ends. Someone deals a new hand. (Comes up with a new intention.) Each new intention makes the players take a risk. They must add more money to the pot in the middle of the table if they want to stay in the game.

Sometimes, as in real life, a character isn't willing to take much of a risk. He folds early and gets out of the game. That, too, signals the end of a beat. A decision to stop, more often than not, forces decisions from other characters that alters their intentions and begins new beats for them. In fact, it's good psychology to string beats together so the pressure rises a bit, backs off a little, and then rises a bit more.

WRITING THE MASTER SCENE

If you read screenwriting contest applications or the guidelines that some producers send to writers, you will see that they want you to work in master scenes. As you recall, I said that master scenes are dramatic action happening at one time, in one place with one set of characters. They also consist of one or more beats that move the plot forward.

Some beginners get confused and try to make every shot an individual scene with its own slug line. But remember the Mad Hatter and the March Hare shrilling at Alice? "Move down. Move down. Clean cup. Clean cup." The poor girl never sat still long enough to drink her tea. Likewise, dramatic action goes haywire when every shot requires a scene change. You must keep the action in one place long enough for the characters to express and pursue their intentions.

If you look at a shooting script, you may see that nearly every shot is a scene. And that's why I said never copy shooting scripts. Again, "calling the shots" is the director's province. Your job is to present a story, set the dramatic action, and develop the character arcs. To that end, you can simply "stay put," perhaps for several pages, playing out your characters' intentions until the beats finish and the master scene concludes. For example:

<u>TIME OUT OF MIND</u>

FADE IN:

EXT. MOUNTAINS - DAY

A green, quiet forest. Mist-shrouded conifers soar skyward. A shaft of golden light falls among them. VALE JAQUITH follows a path that winds tunnel-like beneath the trees. Native American, he is handsome but weather-beaten, a lion who has seen too many battles. His black mane brushing his shoulders, he wears traditional Indian attire. He stares at the light, moving toward it.

The light grows brighter. Two figures emerge. A LITTLE GIRL and an OLD MAN.

                    VALE
          Bonnie? Uncle Eldon?

A third figure, a lovely, dignified WOMAN of 60, emerges.

                    VALE
          Mother?

                    FEMALE VOICE (OS)
          D-fib.

Vale's mother extends her hand to him.

                    MALE VOICE (OS)
          Okay. Clear.

Vale hears electrical PULSES, a BEEP, and a sharp mechanical WHACK. He glances over his shoulder, puzzled. Then, ignoring the sounds, he steps toward the waiting figures.

                    FEMALE VOICE (OS)
          Flat line.

                    MALE VOICE (OS)
          Once more.

The BEEP and WHACK repeat. Again, Vale halts. And this time he turns around.

INT. OFFICE - DAY

Huge windows. A Manhattan skyline. Luxurious furnishings and primitive art. Behind a big desk, a high-back chair faces the windows. An autumn floral arrangement occupies a corner of the desk. ROSS UNGERMAN, mature, good-looking in an efficient sort of way, perches on the other corner. SIBYL HODGE, a secretary, reads from her steno pad.

                          SIBYL
We got a fax from Taiwan.
Negotiation on the ceramics
collection. They want your input.
Your mother called. She'll be
late for lunch. Our contact in
Somalia says the artifacts he
bought won't leave there any time
soon. And--uh--
            (turning a page)
We're ready for your video
conference call with the Indians.

The desk chair swivels to reveal MARGO ERNSDORF. She
has a face that is made for laughter but given more to
frowns.

                          MARGO
Indians?

                          SIBYL
Tribal representatives from Idaho.
Oregon. One of those places where
the deer and the antelope play.

                          MARGO
Why am I meeting with them?

                          SIBYL
They do beadwork. Arrowheads. That
sort of thing.

                          MARGO
Whose bright idea was this?

Sibyl's gaze flicks to the man perched on Margo's desk.

                          SIBYL
Mr. Ungerman.

Margo's eyes follow Sibyl's.

                          MARGO
Ross?

                          ROSS
Margo, my love, things Native
American are trendy.

                          MARGO
Perhaps. But I didn't agree to
confer with Indians.

                    ROSS
          No. You were in Los Angeles. I
          said you'd take the meeting.

                    MARGO
          Ross, you're my manager and my
          fiancé. You are not my CEO.

                    ROSS
          Come on. We're not making a
          treaty with Sitting Bull. We're
          exploring a merchandise source.

She stares at him, lips pursed.

                    ROSS
          If ya don't like their palaver,
          li'l gal, ya can leave 'em in
          Orygone.

She casts her eyes heavenward. And sighs.

                    MARGO
          Okay. Give me a minute to circle
          the wagons.

In the above excerpt, there are two distinct master scenes. Two different locations. Many possible shots. But as a writer, I stick with dramatic action, not how to shoot the film.

The disordering event happens on page 1. In the very first scene, Vale's intention is "going toward the light." He never arrives. With his intention ended, the beat ends. Since we now must move to a new location and a new set of characters, Vale's master scene also ends.

A new master scene begins in Margo's office. It consists of one beat. Her intention is simply to start her work day. But something keeps her from getting what she wants. The beat ends. The next scene will return us to Vale. Change of location. Change of characters. Another master scene and a new beat can begin.

If the action continues in this way, the film will be dramatically correct. But in a good screenplay, a character needs to have increasingly stronger intentions. The character wants more. To get it, (s)he must take bigger risks. Often the stake is money. Or power. Or property. Or love. (Remember your subject and theme statement!) The higher the stakes, the stronger the drama. Of course, the ultimate stake is to bet one's life.

A simple way to motivate characters toward stronger intentions is to threaten what they have. Or at least to write actions the character can interpret as a threat. The brilliant comedian and actor, Danny Thomas, once noted that we don't go to war over what people do. We go to war over what we *think* they will do. An important part of your job is to decide what your characters fear and what they will interpret as a threat.

Some very funny scenes can happen when a character, alone late at night, hears a noise. Maybe just a little noise. The character perhaps has no reason to believe she is in peril. But imagination takes over. And we viewers laugh. We know that fear of being alone in the dark and blowing small things out of proportion are basic parts of human nature. We root for scared people because we have been scared, too. Indeed, we love it when elements increase the tension (more noises). We feel the character's mounting struggle in deciding to take a stand (grabs a baseball bat) and resolve the conflict (throws open the basement door), letting the chips fall where they may.

Using reversals is another way to increase tension. In film, we often see characters lose, but they persist until they triumph. Or for a time a character sails along, getting everything (s)he wants. Then suddenly (s)he loses it all. What will (s)he do? How will (s)he regain power? Such setbacks test the protagonist's mettle. Re-examining goals, (s)he must make new, even braver decisions.

Leave Me Alone! I'm Having a Crisis!

In review, a disordering event causes some kind of threat. A character seeks a solution. If the solution fails, tension increases. The character works harder to find an answer. At last we reach the moment of greatest stress. The irresistible force meets the immovable object. At such times, the character faces a decision that will cause a permanent change in his life. But there is no choice. Decide he must, regardless of the outcome. At that moment, with that decision, a climax occurs.

Moving a story forward through conflict means following the pattern of mounting tension and climax. Sometimes these climaxes will be large; and other times they will be small. The major climaxes, however, occur with your Act One and Act Two turning points. Another occurs at your *midpoint.* In fact, midpoints are so important that a solid one can help compensate for Act One turning points that are a bit soft.

You have only one midpoint. If your script is 120 pages long, this important element should occur in Act Two on page 60 (or as close to it as possible). For protagonists, this is the moment when the struggle peaks. Sometimes called the *point of no return,* it forces protagonists to choose. Will they sink or swim? For at least a brief moment, they seem tempted to sink. They wonder if they made a mistake. They think they can't go on. But then something happens. Something forces them to realize they cannot quit. They must pursue their goals to the (possibly bitter) end.

Unlike a turning point or climax, the midpoint does not require heavy-duty action. As a rule, stronger is better, but midpoints can be fairly quiet. In fact, if the rest of the script has been intense, the contrast of a quiet midpoint can make your midpoint more profound. Just bear in mind that your midpoint must show a moment of ultimate decision. No matter what course the protagonist chooses, life will change forever. In an action film, it may seem that he's cornered and about to die. Forced to take action, thinking he has nothing left to lose, he forms one last new plan and forges ahead.

The protagonist's renewed commitment adds zing to the middle of Act Two just when an audience's interest tends to flag. In the 10 to 15 pages following the midpoint, you need still more action that tests the protagonist's resolve. Now, however, the protagonist is a new person. After the midpoint, doubts vanish. Protagonists enter their strongest "take charge" mode. Win or lose, they become masters of their fate. *Payback,* starring Mel Gibson, has a gut-wrenching midpoint that I believe makes the film.

Some Good Advice

Always follow a dramatic climax with some tranquil moments. Give the audience a breather so they can absorb the full impact of the action. To understand the necessity for such a break, think of how a roller coaster levels off before beginning its new ascent. Think of the knot you get in your stomach as your car again climbs toward the top and another wild descent. You want your audience to feel the same kind of anticipation. A pause after a climax helps you prepare them for the next emotional peak in your story.

THE ACT TWO TURNING POINT

In the first six steps of this book, I said that your Act One turning point can be a bit low key, but Act Two should end with a bang. Well, the moment is here. You are 20 to 30 pages (minutes) away from the ending of your story. One final confrontation, a last disordering event, galvanizes the action and propels the protagonist straight toward resolution. The Act Two turning point is so important that films can succeed or fail based on its effectiveness.

In *Making a Good Script Great,* Linda Seger says the Act Two turning point "speeds up the action. It makes the third act more intense than the other two. It gives a sense of urgency, or momentum, to the story. It pushes the story toward its conclusion."

Act Two turning points take many forms. In the "moment of truth," an incident forces the protagonist to face some reality about himself so he can triumph. *The Sixth Sense* offers a potent "moment of truth" Act Two turning point.

The "reversal" is also common. And strong. The protagonist either turns the tables on someone or gets the tables turned on him. A fine example of an Act Two reversal happens in *The Thomas Crown Affair* starring Pierce Brosnan.

Linda Seger adds: "Sometimes, a second act turning point is a ticking clock— 'Well, James Bond, you have six hours or I blow up Paris!' "

No matter what form of turning point you choose, do your level best to write something original. Fresh. Whenever possible, make it astonish your audience.

EXERCISE 1

1. Log on to the Internet and go to Drew's Script-o-rama:
   http://www.script-o-rama.com/snazzy/dircut.html

   HELPFUL HINT The Internet is an easy place to find scripts free of charge. But if you don't have Internet access, you probably can find it free of charge, at your local public library. Ask the library staff. They will show you how to log on to the site and download the desired files. Or you can go to a company like Kinko's or Lazerquick. For a fee, they will provide the same service.

2. Select 1 (one) first draft or early draft script to download and read. Then, during the coming week, get the matching video and watch the film. Please read the script *before* you watch the film. Also, please choose a film you have *not* seen. Some examples of such scripts that you can find at Drew's include:

My Best Friend's Wedding	*Batman*
Contact	*Entrapment*
Snow Falling on Cedars	*True Lies*
Notting Hill	*8 mm*

WARNING!   Being first or early drafts doesn't mean the above are spec scripts. So, read only for content and writing style. Ignore elements that don't suit spec scripts.

There are many more scripts, plus links to other sites that have first and early drafts of "golden oldies" and recent films. You will be working with your chosen script and film for a few assignments, so choose something that you like and can stick with.

3. Do your standard "laundry list" analysis containing the following:

THE DISORDERING EVENT:

THE PROBLEM THAT MUST BE SOLVED:

THE PROTAGONIST (What makes this person the protagonist?):

THE ANTAGONIST (What makes this person the antagonist?):

A COMPLETE THEME STATEMENT: subject → basic action → goal sentence

THE DRAMATIC PREMISE:

THE ACT ONE TURNING POINT:

THE ACT TWO TURNING POINT:

THE MIDPOINT:

THE MEANS BY WHICH THE PROTAGONIST SOLVES THE PROBLEM:

4. Briefly note the differences you see between the first draft that you read and the finished film. Do the differences surprise you? If so, why?

5. If you have not begun work on Act Two, by all means do so. If you are already working on it, please continue.

All the while, remember:

There is no art without discipline.

There is only chaos.

Chapter **Character Arc**

Creating a character is like becoming a parent. You bring your "infants" into the world, nurture them, and give them space to grow. When they mature, how they turn out is a crapshoot.

Human psychology, with all its complexities, is the root of action. Previously, we talked about methods that you can use to get inside your characters' heads and understand their motivation. Now we'll examine how characters "drive" the plot.

KINDS OF CHARACTERS

So far, you have worked with two primary characters: the protagonist and the antagonist. You know that the protagonist can be (and frequently is) the hero or heroine. The antagonist, likewise, can be the villain, but it is not required. Therefore, we should specify when there is a variation from the traditional view of these roles. Moreover, now we need to add the "third character." In reality, in dramatic lingo, this term can refer to any "secondary" character. Adding one or more opens up your plot.

No rule says you must include more than two characters, but writing drama is easier when you have at least three. Personally, I find my writing really starts to flow when I have five. (Uneven numbers seem to work best.) Often, secondary characters are "catalysts." Their existence makes it easier to keep the action going. One might urge the protagonist to keep fighting, another might spy for the antagonist, and yet another can deliver a message that changes the entire thrust of the story.

In each case, like kids lining up for a game of Red Rover, the protagonist has allies who take his part and help him achieve his goal. These are called *support* or *mirror characters*. The antagonist also has a "support group," known as *opposition* or *counter characters*. Another category is *love-interest* or *romantic characters*.

Examine the examples below:

Movie	Protagonist	Antagonist	Support	Opposition	Love Interest
Hamlet	Hamlet	Claudius	Horatio	Gertrude	Ophelia
As Good as It Gets	Melvin	Simon	Carol	Frank	Carol
My Fair Lady	Henry	Eliza	Pickering	Eliza's father	Freddy

Sometimes secondary characters "double in brass," serving more than one function. For example, a love interest in your primary plot can become the antagonist in your subplot. There are also minor characters, often called *day players* in films. Yes, you need them, but these folks pop in and pop out. You don't need to take much time with them.

Writing Character Biographies

What's the best way to write about people? The best approach (as I keep insisting) is to write what you know. The ideal situation is to look around you. Study the people in your own sphere. Draw parallels between them and your characters. Combining attributes from two or more people in your personal circle, you can create fresh, new composite characters. But by all means, start with people who are real to you. They have the best chance of being real to your audience.

In the first six steps, we used the "Magic If" to get inside a character's head. I love this technique and have fun running the movie in my mind. But other tools might work better for you. When you discover new methods, by all means try them. Screenwriting is a "learn by doing" craft. The more you experiment, the greater your chances to grow.

Some people write character biographies. They create and record every detail about a character, even if they never actually put the information into the script. (In theory, such details reveal the character's psyche and foreshadow his or her relationship to other characters.) Personally, the biography approach turns me off. If I write a minutely detailed account of every character, I won't have enough energy left to write the screenplay. Some people, however, swear by this method. So if you think it might work for you, give it a shot.

By all means, however, bear in mind that character biographies can become too complex. If you go the biography route, be brief. Limit yourself to pertinent data. A way to discipline yourself is to set up a chart that looks like this:

FILM: *As Good as It Gets*

Character: Melvin

HOME & FAMILY	Lives alone. No ties. No strings.
EDUCATION & PRACTICAL SKILLS	Well educated. Intelligent. Imaginative. Articulate.
CAREER AND/OR LIFESTYLE	Writes romance novels.
PERSONALITY TRAITS	Curmudgeon. Is compulsive/obsessive. Does cruel things without realizing the consequences.
PRIMARY INTERESTS	Himself and his illness.

Character: Carol

HOME & FAMILY	Single. Her young son has health problems. Lives with and is close to her mother.

EDUCATION & PRACTICAL SKILLS	Not much education, but intelligent and highly articulate.
CAREER AND/OR LIFESTYLE	Waitress. Wants a social life and romance, but has many problems because of son's illness.
PERSONALITY TRAITS	Responsible. Caring. Independent. Empathetic.
PRIMARY INTERESTS	Her world revolves around her child, but she wants much more.

Just as it did with planning Act One, a simple "laundry list" approach allows you to record many details without writing a book about each character. If there are details you decide you don't like or want to change, it's quick and easy to do so.

Character Development

No doubt at some point in your life an important decision has loomed on your horizon. Perhaps it was a normal and basic choice that most people have to make, like deciding what person to date or what college to attend. Maybe it was a disruptive choice, such as taking a new job in a city far away. Or perhaps you had to make a split-second decision, like meeting another car in terrible traffic and choosing between the brakes or the gas.

Whatever the circumstances, there comes a time in everyone's life when one has to take action, knowing there will be consequences, but not being able to guess at the outcome. So we leap and hope a net will appear. One of our choices may turn out beautifully; another may be an appalling disappointment. Although we may fear confronting obstacles and believe making choices will ruin us, more often we emerge wiser and stronger. So perhaps these encumbrances are best considered the natural evolution of the human soul. Certainly, anything that changed your life forever helped shape you into the person you are today.

Likewise, your characters must confront obstacles. Hard as they try to do what's right, ultimately they, too, must leap and hope, without knowing the outcome. That is how a character, like any other human being, learns and grows. From the first disordering event, your characters make decisions and face consequences that make the character change and grow. This is the *character arc*.

To understand the importance of character arcs in your screenplay, imagine crossing a bridge only to discover it ends in the middle of the river. Now think about following the actions of a protagonist and an antagonist. What if they end in the middle of the story? The events, decisions, and consequences you write for these crucial characters are bridges that must span your entire script.

Remember that character arcs don't simply happen. Beginning at Point A, your protagonist must *decide* to climb emotional mountains, trudge over heartrending deserts, and stave off bandito attacks until he reaches Point Z. Likewise, the antagonist, starting as close as possible to Point A, must *decide* to remove trail markers, poison the water holes, and wait in ambush. Decisions and their consequences are the saddle horses and pack animals that carry the conflict forward.

Study the following examples.

Hamlet

DECISION: Hamlet hires a group of players to reenact old Hamlet's murder before King Claudius to see how the king will react. *(Hamlet: If he but blench, I know my course.)*

CONSEQUENCE: During the play, Claudius grows uncomfortable, revealing his guilt.

DECISION: Hamlet wants to kill Claudius.

French Kiss

DECISION: When her fiancé goes to Paris and falls for someone else, a woman decides to go after him and bring him back.

CONSEQUENCE: On the plane, she meets a rough but charming Frenchman.

DECISION: She enlists the Frenchman's help in making her fiancé jealous.

As Good as It Gets

DECISION: When his artist neighbor's little dog becomes too annoying, Melvin Udall drops the dog down a garbage chute.

CONSEQUENCE: The neighbor's agent says he will make Melvin pay the neighbor back.

DECISION: When the neighbor is hospitalized, Melvin agrees to take care of the dog.

Now ask yourself, "How does the psychology of each character change because of these decision/consequence sequences?" In drama, as in real life, one thing leads to another. Always. When you can track the changes in psychology and behavior that a sequence causes, then you are following the character arc.

KEEPING THE FAITH

A writer controls many things in a script. The given circumstances—meaning the environment in which the play takes place—are completely your choice. Certainly, you choose the disordering event. Above all, you create the characters and launch their dramatic action. In the creation of all these things, you have complete charge. But once you commit your characters to the page, another factor appears: You are honor bound to play them straight. By that, I mean you must retain the identity that you gave them when they were "born." A quick way to alienate an audience is to start with a character who is one kind of person and then suddenly, without warning, that character becomes someone else.

True, life is about being and becoming. And over the course of a film, character arcs show changes. But these changes are the result of learning experiences, not psychotic episodes. Your heroes may discover their dark sides. They must still be heroes. Your villains may regret the error of their ways; they may even reform. But they remain villains. Certainly, you should never turn your hero into a villain. Nor can the villain become your hero.

Some writers think it is devilishly clever to change horses in midstream. Such a jump, however, creates a totally different story that has nowhere to go unless all of the underpinnings—theme statement, premise, and so on—also change. But, you ask, what about the alterations you often see in a character's personality and personal philosophy? A dedicated doctor becomes Rambo. A man who deeply loves his wife plots her destruction. A mean old miser becomes generous. Contradictions in character are permitted and can be very interesting—as long as the writer "sets the stage."

Foreshadowing

When a writer portrays events that prepare the audience for changes in the characters (and therefore the plot), it is called *foreshadowing*. Such clues can be broad and obvious, but just as often they are subtle. Perhaps it is a line in an action paragraph or a few words of dialogue. A shot of a clock foreshadows a story in which time is essential. A window accidentally left open foreshadows a burglar's raid. A woman's departure from a doctor's office can foreshadow all kinds of things. If she is laughing, it can mean something wonderful. If she bursts into tears, the audience braces for bad news. A ball bouncing across a road can warn us of impending danger for a child.

But while you work, bear in mind that strong emphasis on any detail creates expectations with the audience. In fact, *every* detail you include creates expectations with the audience. They assume the detail must be important, or you would not point it out. The more you "play up" an aspect, the higher the audience's expectations will be.

Now, because you're quick and perceptive, you say to yourself, "Oh, *that's* why she wants us to omit extraneous details." Yes! That's one reason. Save yourself and the audience a lot of frustration. Write *only* what you need. When you find details that are not important to your story, prune them. Ruthlessly.

More Helpful Hints

To help the audience follow the character arc, we need to foreshadow any events that are likely to alter a character's behavior. For example, let's say we meet a doctor who is in the military. But he abhors military life, and he's delighted when he gets his discharge. Then several scenes later, he is at a hospital, becoming a hostage with cruel captors who murder innocent victims. Showing him first as a military man foreshadows the possibility that he will turn into Rambo.

Likewise, if we first learn that a wife hired a hit man to kill her husband, we can understand a loving husband who turns vengeful. When we see that Scrooge was once a kind, loving person, we can better accept him becoming that way again. It's about preparation. And motivation. Knowing your itinerary before you embark. Planning events and behavior before you write.

Treat Your Characters as if They Are Real People

There are things you might say to your father that you'd never say to your mother. There are places you'd take your best friend, but you'd never take your significant other. You might fib to your boss, but you'd never lie to an IRS agent. Consider the "real" people around you and how you deal with them. Approach your characters the same way.

Put "Teeth" into Your Consequences

If the piper must be paid, get out your checkbook. Do not waver. Never fade. When you feel affection for your characters, following through on logical consequences can be difficult.

I once wrote a script that had three characters I adored. As work progressed, however, my only reasonable option was for one character to die. These people felt very real to me. I could not conceive of "killing" one. I put the script away, thinking I would find an alternate solution. It is still waiting. To wimp out and save the character would lessen the story's impact. Instead, I chose not to complete it. Of course, this is an extreme case. But it is a good illustration, I think. Sometimes you are like a general sending troops into battle, and there will be casualties.

Play against Audience Expectations

Earlier, I said that a solution for predictability is to choose behavior for your character that is logical but off-beat and/or inappropriate. For example, with Melvin Udall and his neighbor's dog, Melvin's options were:

1. Knock on his neighbor's door and complain.
2. Call the building manager and complain.
3. Call animal control and complain.
4. Drop the dog down the garbage chute.

The first three are definitely predictable. But did the audience think Melvin would drop that little dog down the garbage chute? Of course not! And could they possibly guess where such "off the wall" behavior would lead? No way!

Another surprise for the audience is to let a minor decision have earthshaking consequences. For instance, let's say that our protagonist wants onions on his hamburger. Hardly a monumental choice. But what if his girlfriend hates onion breath? What if they quarrel and she leaves? What if the waitress at the hamburger joint gives him a wink with his fries? In that case, a burger with onions can change the protagonist's life.

Indeed, strong disordering events can arise from this concept. For instance, a man decides to leave his car at home and walk to work. No big deal. But on the way, he witnesses a bank heist. Or a conservative woman decides to buy a flashy dress. And for the first time in years, her husband is turned on. The possibilities are endless!

Play against Character Stereotypes

This technique also helps you break away from character stereotypes. For instance:

1. A wimpy nerd drives race cars.
2. A child has the body of an adult.

3. A secret agent is clumsy and inept.

4. A lounge singer masquerades as a nun.

WARNING!   Remember you can't pull things out of the air. When you play against audience expectations, your material must remain reasonable and logical. To achieve that goal, always motivate your characters from within, using the Magic If. Then give hints and clues that foreshadow changes so the audience can accept them.

EXERCISE 2

1. Carefully review the first draft screenplay you downloaded from the Internet.

2. View the films *As Good as It Gets* and *City of Angels.* (I found *As Good as It Gets* on Drew's Script-o-rama. I don't know what draft it is. But you're more than welcome to read the script.)

3. Copy the form below onto a sheet of paper. List characters from each film in the appropriate categories.

Movie	Protagonist	Antagonist	Support	Opposition	Love Interest
Your Film Choice					
As Good as It Gets					
City of Angels					

4. Copy the following form onto a sheet of paper. Make one for each of the films you viewed. Beginning with the disordering event, track the *protagonist character arc* for each of the assigned screenplays.

    YOUR FILM CHOICE: Protagonist _____

DECISION	CONSEQUENCE	CHANGE
1.		
2.		
3.		
4.		
5.		

5. For each of the above stories, use your imagination and try to create at least one (1) *alternate* decision, consequence, and change for the protagonist. How do you think your change will affect the story? Do you think it will strengthen the story? Why? Why not? (If you find more than five or want to write more than one change, feel free! The more work you do, the faster you grow.)

Chapter 3 Subplot

Most events in our lives cause or lead to other events. In screenwriting, we chain a series of events together to add depth and substance.

By itself, your primary plot sets its focus on a central struggle between two characters. That can be interesting, but it gives your characters a limited playing field. What about those intriguing layers that you want? To get them, often you need to create dramatic action that involves events with other characters. The solution is to launch a subplot.

A *subplot* is a supporting storyline that arises from and/or spins off your primary plot. Since everything in dramatic material is based on people DO-ing to each other, subplots give characters more room in which to do it. The trick is to include the darn things without letting them run you ragged.

One main subplot is par. You can add others—for total of three to five—that run throughout your script. Frankly, though, this is not a case of "the more the merrier." Each additional storyline must be developed and concluded, much like your main plot. Likewise, the audience must be able to follow and understand each subplot. To juggle five storylines in two hours is definitely a challenge. More than five would be madness.

Generally, subplots begin during Act One. In classes, however, I avoid discussing them with introductory students. You must learn to walk before you can run. Until beginners can nail the concept of launching a strong central plot, adding subplots can turn the story landscape into a quagmire. But now, of course, you have become an expert. (Wink. Smile.) So we can move on.

THE "A" STORY AND THE "B" STORY

Behold! You see above perhaps the most confusing buzzwords in Hollywood! Really, of course, the title of this section refers to plot and subplot. Logically, the *A story* is your central conflict. The *B story,* then, is the main subplot. But brace yourself for a bit of screenwriting irony.

You expect the A story to be more important and powerful than the B story, but sometimes it isn't. Just as the terms *protagonist* and *antagonist* have nothing to do with a character's morals, alphabetical placement of storylines does *not* determine their power. The A story, the outward struggle, is like the framework of a house, whereas the B story, the subplot, is like a window that lets us see into a character's soul.

Sometimes the Subplot Rules!

Or so it seems. Let's say your protagonist is an environmentalist fighting city hall. He wants the mayor to stop air pollution. That's the A story. The central question is, "Will Joe make Mayor Brassbuttons stop air pollution?" Then, however, Joe meets the mayor's beautiful daughter, Esmeralda. They fall in love. That's the B story. It is entirely possible—and often happens—that the lovers' tale will become more important to the audience than the protagonist's struggle against the "bad guys," the system, or whatever.

In *Donovan's Reef,* John Wayne is a tough-guy protagonist facing a tough-gal antagonist. But Donovan's relationship with the film's children shows a big heart beating beneath his thick hide. That B story gives Donovan a chance to reveal his true self, true feelings, and/or true love. As a rule, of course, the B story stays in the background. But in some films, the A story fades into insignificance, nearly forgotten, while the B story plays out. Then the A story rises again at the end of the film to tie up loose ends.

Isn't the Subplot Just Another Plot?

Well, yes and no. (Don't you love it when I'm succinct?) A subplot has the same basic dramatic structure as a primary plot. A beginning, middle, and end. A disordering event. A problem to be solved. A protagonist. An antagonist. But there are important differences:

1. *Every major character involved with the primary plot can initiate a subplot.* The key words are *major character* and *involved.* Subplots often give the supporting or counter characters and the love interests their own storylines within the main plot. But don't worry about every waiter, cab driver, or cop on the beat. Focus on the characters who are visible long enough for a subplot to develop.

2. *A subplot will always depend upon the primary plot.* Think of the song lyrics that admonish, "Lean on me when you're not strong, . . ." That's a good analogy for what happens between a central plot and a subplot. Figuratively, the Joe-and-Esmeralda story "leans" on the environmentalist story. If Joe has a sidekick, a street sweeper named Horace, there could be a Joe and Horace story. The central conflict could support a Mayor-Brassbuttons-and-his-evil-assistant story. So now you have three subplots waiting for your attention. However . . .

3. *A subplot tends to be less complete than a primary plot.* If you separate the central plot from a subplot, and try to read the subplot as an independent piece of material, the subplot probably won't stand alone—at least not without major revisions and additions. But its existence broadens the central plot, adds depth to it, and gives it more "oomph." It adds the famous "layers" I've talked about so much.

4. *You can cut back and forth between the primary plot and a subplot.* You don't have to follow the protagonist around. Give Joe a break. Leave him off screen for a few scenes while Esmeralda dines with her father and challenges the old man on Joe's behalf.

5. *Some sources advocate different protagonists and antagonists in subplots.* In my experience, a subplot's protagonist will be the same as the protagonist in your primary plot. But I

believe the antagonist can change. There's no rule, so you must decide what works best for you. As I mentioned in the first six steps, however, subplots can cause confusion about what characters, or how many characters, fulfill these functions in a film. To sort out your subplots, look for *one* protagonist and antagonist with one central conflict *per storyline.*

Critical Decisions

Sometimes a writer weaves main plot and subplot together so skillfully that they seem equally strong. Indeed, even the audience may have a hard time deciding which is the A story and which is the B story.

What about you, the struggling writer? How can you judge which is which? Sometimes you can't. In fact, one of my biggest surprises came when I mistook a subplot for my central plot. I could see the script wasn't working, but I didn't know why. It took a review from a savvy friend to spot the problem.

How can you avoid it? Rely on good planning! Use every tool I've given you. For each subordinate story, write a theme statement and a dramatic premise. (You know the drill.) Use visual aids. Some people like notecards. Some like tables and flowcharts. Anything that shows subplot development can help keep you organized.

Still, even with your best efforts, being close to your work can cloud your thinking. Another valuable asset is to have an honest friend with a good literary sense to review your material and tell you candidly what he or she sees. If your reader can follow your storylines easily, you probably are doing well. If not, go back to the drawing board.

Subplot Function

If you have ever driven across the Great Plains on a highway that stretches endlessly toward the horizon without a bend or curve, you know how boring straight lines can be. Yet, another road that intersects the highway can pique your curiosity—especially when it leads to structures or geographic features on another horizon. You wonder where the intersecting road leads. And what would happen if you were to follow it.

Subplots do the same thing. A central plot tends to be linear. Stretching straight ahead of you. True, a subplot can run parallel to the central plot, thereby reinforcing it, but a subplot also can be a rest stop that gives the audience a breather. Or it can be a detour that complicates the overall journey.

Let's take a film that actually deals with a journey. In *The Straight Story,* the protagonist, an elderly man, learns that his brother, from whom he is alienated, had a stroke. The protagonist wants to see his brother before it is too late. But the brother, the antagonist, lives far away. The protagonist can barely walk. He can't drive. And there's no bus to his destination. So he decides to drive his garden tractor. That is the A story.

This example is not exactly a rip-roaring tale. Indeed, this could be one of the dullest films on record. But soon, subplots intersect the old geezer's linear highway. He meets people, and they meet him. These folks connect and bring something to each other's lives. A warm, sweet adventure with stellar performances, the film is a fine visual metaphor about the journey of life. And, through its subplots, the film reassures us that humanity is alive and well.

When you integrate your subplots therefore, the most crucial aspect is *connection.* You must decide carefully when and how your subplot will meet your central conflict. Will you have two parallel stories, skipping back and forth between them? Will you surprise your audience with a detour that finally loops back to the main road? Or will you let your central plot "ride" on a subplot, distracting the audience while you prepare for bold new central plot action? Whatever your decision, the key is to plan and play out your subplot just as carefully as you do your primary plot.

THE ACID TEST

All of the tests you have used for your primary plot apply equally to subplots. But perhaps the best test is to define what your subplot will add to the story. A good method is to use the following sentence and fill in the blanks:

"This script is not only about _____ but it is also about

_____ ."

For *ET,* you might say, "This script is not only about aliens discovering our world but it is also about making friends." For *Fly Away Home,* you might say, "This film is not only about a girl who reconciles with her father but it is also about gaining independence."

This step clarifies your subplot's place in the general scheme of your script. It also gives you a jump start on your subplot theme statement. In short, it helps you decide how your subplot relates to and affects your main plot.

EXERCISE 3

Returning to the screenplays you have been assigned so far, do the following for each:

1. Apply the above acid test to each of the assigned screenplays. Write the results.

2. Prepare a "laundry list" analysis that identifies the A story and B story of each film. Include the usual elements: disordering event, theme statement, protagonist, antagonist, and central question for *both* the A story *and* the B story.

Chapter 4 — Subtext

You've heard these phrases all your life: A picture is worth a thousand words. Actions speak louder than words. But if you write screenplays, those platitudes become your primer.

Human awareness is easily jaded. Simple recognition doesn't interest us. We expect it. We gravitate to surprises. For example, in farm country, the sight of a big red barn won't hold our attention for long. On the other hand, if the barn stands on rickety timbers in the midst of filth, we might take a second look (shaking our heads in dismay). But what if the same barn has JESUS SAVES painted in huge, pure white letters on the roof?

No, I'm not being sacrilegious. I grew up in farm country, and there was such a barn. The owners were devoted to their Christian faith, if not to their house . . . er . . . barn keeping. Passersby would stop and stare, incredulous at the combination of squalor and holiness. It was my first exposure to the impact of visual images. Today, of course, thanks to film and television, we're bombarded with them. To write a successful screenplay, you must understand how to construct them.

Just as painters create pictures that communicate ideas and provoke thought, so do writers. Instead of pigment on canvas, however, our medium is action on a screen that is 20 feet high and 50 feet wide. When we augment a simple entity so it stirs aesthetic senses, communicates an idea, and provokes thought, we create a work of art. Therefore, what we create is less important than making sure our creation has meaning. In this pursuit, perhaps our best tool is *subtext.*

Synonyms for *subtext* are *nuance, suggestion, implication, association, undertone,* and *overtone.* In film, to show things exactly as they are or to have characters say exactly what they mean is called being *on the nose.* Much of your script is bound to be on the nose. There's no way to avoid it. But the strongest moments in your screenplay will be those that add intriguing layers of nuance, suggestion, implication, association, undertone, and overtone. Primarily, you present subtext in three ways: visual, action, and dialogue.

VISUAL METAPHOR

Human beings are highly visual creatures, and visual metaphor is the concept of one picture being worth a thousand words. When you write a visual metaphor, the image on the screen will have a special, underlying meaning. This harkens back to the days when films did not have dialogue. They were only images on a screen. Therefore, the images alone had to reveal everything the filmmaker wanted the audience to know. When the talkies arrived, dialogue expanded film's capacity for delivering more precise interpretations. But dialogue has never replaced visual images—especially visual metaphors—in screenplays. I doubt that it ever will.

It's one of the biggest challenges a novice screenwriter faces: to compose strong visual images that convey particular meanings, completely without words. When we succeed, the results approach poetry.

City of Angels offers many such visual metaphors about its characters and their situation. For instance, when Maggie, the antagonist, first appears on the screen. The scene is in a city. A construction site. The streets are torn up. There are potholes. Broken concrete. Barricades. Stalled cars sit bumper to bumper. Then . . .

A bicycle emerges from the traffic. The rider, a slim, fragile-looking woman, weaves in and out of the stalled vehicles, bypassing the chaos.

Arriving at a hospital, she jumps off her bike, wheels it through a service entrance and, a moment later, reappears in a locker room. Her bike helmet and Nikes come off. She dons hospital scrubs. Her beeper sounds. She checks it and dashes off.

Making her way to an operating room, she completes a transformation that reveals she is a heart surgeon.

If we were storytelling instead of story DO-ing, a nurse or an orderly might see her coming and say, "There's Maggie. She's a heart surgeon." That would be narration. Plain. Clunky. Boring. Instead, a vivid image of Maggie riding her bike tweaks the viewer's brain. As well, her journey through the construction site and traffic jam offers intriguing clues about her personality as well as her profession.

First, a woman riding a bike through heavy traffic displays a vigorous and intrepid spirit. Especially when she could just as easily lounge in a BMW with a vanilla latte and the air conditioning going full tilt.

Second, what does a heart surgeon *do?* Goes to a medical construction site (operating room). Weaves in and out of damaged bodies. Deals with stalled organs. Bypasses chaos. Repairs damage.

See how that works? The visual metaphor speaks volumes, saying far more than many pages of description. Instead of hearing about Maggie from a third party *(boring),* we see her behavior *(stimulating).* Indeed, the character quickly captivates the audience when we see her go from undaunted commuter to dedicated cardiologist.

 ## ACTION SUBTEXT

This kind of subtext is the classic case of actions speaking louder than words. It deals with double meaning in what your characters do.

If you've watched *M.A.S.H.* you might have seen the characters gathered around a table, playing cards and joking with each other while bombs fall outside.

Grosse Point Blank, a "dark" comedy, opens with a contract killer about to do a job. Yet, his behavior is casual and matter of fact—like a normal business man in the course of a normal work day.

In *Amistad,* while the ship twists and turns in violent seas, a woman gives birth. Straining against their chains, the slaves raise up the newborn, passing it from hand to hand, hearing its first cries as if the sound is a kind of anthem. Out of the womb, held above the crush of surrounding humanity, for a moment the baby is free.

Later, the mother, her baby in her arms, stands on deck, witnessing the hell that awaits her and her child as slaves. Her face a mask, she glances over her shoulder at the ocean. Then she steps back and slips over the rail, choosing death for them both.

Poet Edgar Lee Masters wrote, "We are voiceless in the face of realities. We cannot speak." Many times in life an emotional event takes away our words. All we can do is stand blinking. Or open our arms to another person. Or perhaps turn away, overwhelmed.

The World Trade Center disaster was such an event. The actions that cameras captured on that dreadful day defy words and render them puny. When we see what people did, only then can we truly understand.

Action subtext expresses a deeper, more complex meaning than words can convey. Things simply are not what they seem. They might be more than they seem, or less than they seem. But the action on the screen shows something distinctive about the characters and their situation that words simply cannot convey.

DIALOGUE SUBTEXT

It's a peculiar human trait that people often say things they don't mean or find themselves struggling to say exactly what they do mean. Sometimes the problem has a cultural bias. In the United States, if you meet a man who has a bad cold, a polite greeting is, "How are you?" A polite answer is, "Fine." Never mind if you don't care how the guy feels nor that he wants say he is sick as a dog. Good manners sometimes require us to say certain words, even if we don't mean them.

That kind of dialogue subtext is one of the most common, but not the most significant. Often, we struggle with speech because emotions compel us to hold back. Perhaps we feel embarrassed about speaking candidly because it makes us feel vulnerable to bear our souls. Another reason we may hesitate is that we fear the response.

In *Fiddler on the Roof,* Tevye asks, "Do you love me?" to which Golde replies indignantly, "I'm your wife." He repeats the question. She remains evasive. He persists. It's pulling teeth, but finally she admits, "I suppose I do." Then the two of them conclude, "It doesn't change a thing, but after 25 years, it's nice to know." It's one of the most poignant and delightful moments in musical theater.

In *City of Angels,* when a patient dies on her table, Maggie must tell his family. Trying to project a professional demeanor, she can't bring herself to say the awful words. She buries them in medical terminology, which confuses the family. At last, Maggie stammers, "He didn't survive." The family collapses in agony, and Maggie finds a solitary place to cry. With her professional façade stripped away, we understand that she is a caring person with huge conscience and a tender heart. (Seth, of course, sees it, too!)

When Harry Met Sally shows the couple in a cafe. At first, the scene appears to be pretty much "on the nose." Sally says she can fake an orgasm. Harry says she can't. Loudly, with total aplomb, she proves him wrong. Her subtext, however, is to turn him on, which, judging from his expression, she does quite well. Moreover, a woman at another table tells the waiter, "I'll have what she's having." Wow! Talk about subtext!

The TV series *West Wing* involves a U.S. president and his staff trying to run the nation. One episode dealt with the president facing the issue of capital punishment. Will he commute a killer's death sentence? It's a choice only he can make, but his staff tries to help. In the process, they discover their own ambivalence. Among others, his press secretary notes that if the execution happens she must make the public announcement. She has never met the accused, and given the brutal nature of his crimes, she has little reason to care about him. "I just wish," she adds with a sigh, "that I didn't know his mother's name is Sophia." It's stunning subtext we all can admire.

 # TRUST YOUR AUDIENCE

Okay. Picture this:

```
EXT. GRAND CANYON - DAY

Decked in climbing gear, MIKE and MONA cling to a cliff.
Mike reaches for a ledge. Stones shower down.

                    MIKE
          Some loose rock here.

Mona glances at the ledge and nods.

                    MIKE
          You have to be careful.

He points to the ledge.

                    MIKE
          It could be dangerous.
```

The beat occurs in a precarious location with action and dialogue subtext that clearly indicate *danger.* Mona sees and acknowledges the problem. For all of that, Mike offers three "on the nose" warnings. But this is film. The audience sees and hears everything. When visual images and subtext project a meaning that viewers can readily follow, *why* do writers feel compelled to spell out the action?

Rent *The Grass Harp* and watch it with a critical eye. Do a "laundry list" analysis. Then tell me, does this movie give you a migraine? If so, you're in good company.

Basing the script on Truman Capote's novel, the filmmakers tried to keep Capote's rich narrative prose as well as his sterling characters. Unfortunately, they did justice to neither. In particular, Act One suffers from voice-over narrative which explains:

1. What the audience will see
2. What the audience is seeing
3. What the audience just saw

Throughout Act One, backstory rules, and major points are explained at least three times. It takes 40 long minutes for the audience to realize the young central character is not the protagonist. In fact, the central character's aunt owns the problem of the play, and therefore the central conflict. Should an audience have to wait 40 minutes to find out who is the protagonist? I vote no.

In fact, for *The Grass Harp,* most of the backstory can be cut simply by changing the point of attack. The voice-over can be trimmed to a few poignant lines. (Please, people, use voice-over *only* when it adds something special that furthers the action.) Act One could be 20 minutes of brisk dramatic action rather than 40 minutes of "talking heads" information that puts my students to sleep every time I show the film.

The visuals are terrific. Subtext is present. The best actors in the business grace the cast. But the folks who made this film doubt their audience. They think we aren't smart enough or sophisticated enough to "fill in the blanks." They must explain the action to us. Over and over. Until we want to gag.

True. No matter how well you write, there will be someone in your audience who doesn't "get it." But you can't cater to the lowest level of viewer. Nowadays, you live in a world where audiences have cut their teeth on everything from *Lord of the Rings* and *A Beautiful Mind* to *Shakespeare in Love.* Trust them. Go for subtext!

EXERCISE 4

1. In each of the films assigned earlier, find and write down at least three additional examples of visual metaphor, action subtext, and dialogue subtext. For each example, state briefly what you think the subtext means.

    HELPFUL HINT   Get in the habit of doing this exercise (and others) whenever you watch films. Just be kind. Do it silently, in your head, so you don't disturb others who may be watching the film with you. (My family threatens to tar and feather me if I do one more analysis aloud while they are present.)

2. In your own screenplay (or one of them), find and list at least three examples of the same elements. Write down what you believe your subtext means.

Chapter 5 · Act Three

This is the moment your audience has been waiting for. Your crowning achievement. The final 20 to 30 pages that make your first 80 or 90 pages worthwhile.

Imagine that you are climbing Mt. Everest. At last you get within reach of the summit. But then you stop. In fact, despite all the investment of time and emotion, not to mention money, you break camp and go back down the mountain. That's the disheartening experience an audience gets when a writer falters in Act Three. The answer, of course, is to complete your story with all the energy you can muster.

Sadly, after vigorously writing two acts the writer's flow of creativity can dwindle to a trickle, leaving the characters high and dry. Writers want to finish the race, but, like marathon runners, they hit a wall. Hard work serves no purpose if the audience grumbles, "Good story, but it falls apart at the end."

THE LAST HURRAH

David Mamet says, "It's important to remember that it is not the dramatist's task to create confrontation or chaos but, rather, to create order." From the beginning, your protagonist searches for answers that will restore order to her world and life. Obstacles detain and frustrate her. Unsure, she falters. At the end of Act Two, she faces a hurdle so big it nearly defeats her. But she decides to carry on.

Act Three, the last 20 to 25 pages of text, marks what some people call "the final push" and "the big finish." Here you will conclude the action, tie up your loose ends, and "pay off" the audience.

Show the Protagonist Solving the Problem

In his quest for a solution, the protagonist tries various plans. Each one fails. The experience, however, changes him in some way. In fact, the changes give him new determination. Putting one last plan into motion, he faces his final obstacle. Like a thoroughbred in a steeplechase, he gathers his strength. The climax comes when the protagonist either succeeds or fails.

In *City of Angels,* Seth knows he wants Maggie and wants to share his life with her. But she rejects the idea of an angel as her lover. And she does not want the responsibility for what will happen to him if he falls. Ignoring her reluctance, he chooses to fall (the ultimate decision). Forever changed (from angel to mortal), he finds himself in a strange world. He has no identity. He has no knowledge of things we mortals take for granted, such as money, transportation, and technology.

Worse, when Seth finally arrives at the hospital, Maggie is gone. Naive as a child, Seth faces one final obstacle. He doesn't know where to go nor how to reach Maggie, but he must find her. Each mile he travels tests his resolve and saps his strength (the final push). Yet, he presses on until at last he reaches Maggie's door (and the dramatic climax of the story). Will Seth win Maggie's love? Will she accept him as a man? Will he share her life? She opens the door. In the audience's mind, her appearance raises the central question one last time: Will Seth share Maggie's life?

When Maggie sees Seth and realizes he is human, the question is answered. The characters and the audience hit the emotional peak of the story. From that moment, the plot moves toward final resolution (also called *denouement*). True, in this film the writer gives the resolution an ironic twist that basically un-answers the central question. But never mind.

Completing Themes and Character Relationships

To me, the central question for *City of Angels* is: Will Seth win Maggie's love? The answer is yes. And no.

One could say this film's underlying principle is, "Be careful what you fall for. You might get it." The story includes the element of the hero with a tragic flaw. Seth sacrifices all for Maggie. They share a brief, joyous interval. And then she is gone. But what does the story really mean? Love → losing? No. In this film, whose mood closely parallels *What Dreams May Come,* I think the theme statement should read:

love → winning

Despite the risks, Seth wants to win Maggie's love.

Seth has hope in the face of adversity, he keeps faith with Maggie, and he loves her against all odds. Ultimately, however, he learns that life is fragile and there are no guarantees, which gives the ending a bereft, disturbing note. Yet in a deeper sense, I think the story means that hope, faith, and love should not be blind. When we do something, we must understand what we are getting into and take responsibility for it. Since those elements are presented effectively, I think Act Three of *City of Angels* completes its theme and plays out its character relationships very well.

"Pay Off" the Audience

Did you ever walk out of a theater or away from your TV set with scenes still playing in your mind? Days, weeks, maybe months later, do you still feel a tug at your heart when you remember moments from a particular film?

Some movies are such a delight that you don't want to forget them. For me, that means films like *The Quiet Man, My Fair Lady, Ghost,* and *Dances with Wolves.* to name a few. Some movies are very hard to watch, but their emotional impact is so great and they pay off so well that we can't forget them. *Saving Private Ryan, The Hours,* and *The Piano Player* will haunt you long after the screen goes dark. If they ended with a whimper, however, we would forget them. Knowing how to leave the audience with a sense of satisfaction and awe is one of the most important skills screenwriters cultivate.

What do you want the people in your audience to know that they didn't know before they entered the theater? What do you want them to feel? That's what all your work comes down to. A good ending is one that seems right and proper for the emotions you help the audience experience. A wonderful ending makes them leave the theater believing you gave them much more.

ENDINGS TO AVOID

The Famous-Detective Solution

A famous detective realizes "whodunnit." So he gathers the characters together, explains how the crime was committed, and names the culprit. Indeed, we expect this ritual from Perry Mason, Jessica Fletcher, or Hercule Poirot. Although these folks certainly entertain us, do their recited facts give you goose bumps?

On the other hand, what happens to the hair on the back of your neck when Dirty Harry ferrets out a criminal and snarls, "Go ahead! Make my day!"

Yes, folks. Dramatic action empowers your work. Every time.

Although you can get away with the Famous Detective Solution in a crime drama, imagine that *City of Angels* ends with Seth explaining to Cassiel what happened between him and Maggie. Or suppose the dramatic climax of *As Good as It Gets* consists of Melvin sitting in the cafe reciting what happened between himself and Carol to the other diners.

Explained endings bring the words *boring* and *snoring* immediately to mind. Yes, you may need a few expository lines to complete your story, but be careful. Write the strongest action you can muster. Then weave in your expository lines sparingly to make them plausible and palatable.

The Bolt-Out-of-the-Blue Solution

After building the protagonist/antagonist struggle to a fever pitch, someone else jumps in or something suddenly happens that solves the problem of the play. All of us have seen such endings. And most of us have wondered what possessed the writer.

In the worst possible scenario, the protagonist is locked in mortal combat. Cornered, he is on the brink of death. Suddenly a shot rings out. The assassin crumbles. The protagonist is saved. Where did the shot come from? A supporting character or, horror of horrors, a character we have never seen before, fires the fatal shot. In a variation, the protagonist gets trapped with nowhere to turn. Some wondrous force, ranging from sheer coincidence to space aliens or the Voice of God, suddenly provides a solution. Characters begin proclaiming, "It's a miracle!"—and the audience groans.

Some writers mistake such travesties for "surprise" endings. But there is a huge difference between surprise and schlock. Far from being clever, lightning-bolt endings tend to be shamelessly manipulative. They can embarrass the audience, making them feel cheated. Such endings can even rate a hearty laugh when it's the last thing a writer wants.

Always remember that the protagonist owns the problem of the play. He or she must solve it. That is what you have prepared the audience for, so that is what the audience *wants*. For a writer to snatch away that opportunity renders the protagonist passive and weak. Worse, it can turn a good story into a joke.

The Pot-of-Gold Solution

Pot-of-gold solutions give films happy endings. In fact, you can give the most somber drama a happy ending. The question is, *should* you? Does every script need one?

Most people prefer happy endings, but writers can't become slaves to them. Certainly, audiences do not require happy endings; they simply want to feel that the ending is appropriate for the story you provide. In fact, viewers tend to become cranky if you pave the way for the tragic death of your protagonist but let him walk away with the girl.

The audience does not know your meaning in advance. Based on the behavior you let them see and hear, they decipher your meaning. In Act Three, the audience must make its final decision. Perhaps you intend them to see, "There's a pot of gold at the end of the rainbow." Or perhaps you want them to think, "Life is not all pansies and primroses." At any rate, you must know your meaning and carry it through to the end. If that gives you room for a happy ending, fine. If not, remember you have a responsibility to write the *truth*. Write a happy ending honestly because your story needs one and it will satisfy your audience, not because you think it is safe and/or expected of you.

 # THE BIG FINISH

Here are some endings that you might want to cultivate.

The One-and-Only Solution

This type of ending is inevitable. In fact, if viewers don't get the results they expect, they probably will picket the box office. Certainly, a screenwriter who does a film about the British winning the American Revolution better have his passport in order.

When we watch James Bond, Indiana Jones, or Batman, our hearts may be in our mouths while they fight the enemy, but we know they will win. Films based on familiar tales such as *Ever After* or fantasies such as *What Dreams May Come* can spin us through marvelous, even startling worlds. But before the final credits roll, we know the protagonist will triumph.

Sometimes we know how the story ends before we enter the theater. *The Diary of Anne Frank, Titanic, Patch Adams,* and wacky, off-beat *Fargo* represent very different plots and productions. But these pieces are fact and/or historically based, so they do not bother with alternate endings. For such films, the entertainment value comes from watching the characters entangle and then extricate themselves. The excitement comes from well-developed, credible characters and strong dramatic action.

The Big-Bang Solution

These are true surprise endings, and they can be hard to write. Modern audiences watch lots of film and television. They have seen all the basic stories in various incarnations thousands of times. By Act Three, they probably suspect how your story will end. (Who can watch a romantic comedy and not believe the guy and gal will get together?)

Personally, I adore surprise endings, but very few films leave me saying, "Hey, I didn't see that coming." Over the years, those that did include *Laura, Psycho* (of course), *Thelma and Louise, Life Is Beautiful,* and *The Sixth Sense.* What grabs one person may not grab another, so probably you have a list of your own. But I think you will agree that when they work, surprise endings are great.

Like illusions by Penn and Teller, surprise endings are masterpieces of *misdirection.* The story takes us down the wrong path, here a red herring, there a red herring. The writer reveals just enough to lead us to the wrong conclusion, yet not enough to make us suspicious. Some popular "misdirecting" devices are:

> **HIDE IN PLAIN SIGHT.** (The protagonist overlooks the obvious.)
>
> **THE LEAST LIKELY SUSPECT.** (Who would have thought the grandmother did it?)
>
> **LOST IN A CROWD.** (The solution is masked in a sea of faces.)

Presumed Innocent uses these devices to good effect. I knew the protagonist didn't do the murder. (Harrison Ford a murderer? No way!) In about the middle of Act Two, I spotted the real culprit because there were no others who could compete. Offering one or two additional suspects might have sustained the illusion.

It's wise to bear in mind that surprise situations don't necessarily cause surprise endings. In *Double Jeopardy* a woman convicted of killing her husband discovers he is still alive. Under the law, she can't be tried for the same crime twice. So once she's out of jail, she can kill him for real, without fear of punishment. An intriguing premise. But I never believed the character—let alone Ashley Judd—could be a killer. (Ms. Judd is a fine actress, but she's neither Betty Davis nor Joan Crawford.) And the film ended exactly as I expected.

Entrapment has a female insurance investigator and a male master thief engaged in a double–double-cross (not to mention a lot of hanky-panky). But you know early on that they are double-crossing each other, so the ending is quite predictable. The fun is watching these indomitable characters dare, court, woo, and twit each other.

Sometimes, when trying to get a surprise ending, writers drag out the climax and resolution. When your audience knows the outcome, such delays are like TV commercials for kitchen gadgets, "But wait! We're not done yet! Keep watching, and we'll give you another twist!" That kind of manipulation can spoil a good film. The ending of *Entrapment* made me feel I'd been played like a fish on a hook. I did enjoy the picture. But I would have preferred an ending that was clean and precise.

The Secret of Success

Of course, the very best ending is the one that works. That means, above all, giving the audience an honest, appropriate outcome that satisfies *them.*

For me, a case in point is the Oscar winner, *Life Is Beautiful.* This amazing film mingles human emotions with great skill. Warm comedy parallels profound tragedy, just as it does in the real world. In the last moments, a clever, loving father makes a supreme sacrifice. Simultaneously, he seems to grant his young son's fondest wish.

In its skillful juxtaposition of joy and sorrow, I think *Life Is Beautiful* has one of the best endings I have seen. Some people criticize this picture for being unrealistic. They insist it has a pot-of-gold ending. Okay. Granted. Endings are in the eye of the beholder. And what works for me may not work for you. This brings us to the element of *artistic taste.*

THE TEACHER'S LAST GASP

Taste. Sometimes it's truly an expression of our inner vision. But there's a flip side. We all remember the housekeeper who tells her prospective employer, "I don't do windows." That's a real challenge for an employer who wants his windows done.

Likewise, the phrase "That's not to my taste" can become a steadfast reason for screenwriting students not to learn dramatic fundamentals. Instead, the students continue doing things the way they always have (while complaining they can't get anyone to read their material, let alone make an offer for it).

Just to mention this subject usually puts students on the defensive, so I postpone the lecture as long as I can. But, gosh, folks, we're approaching the end of the book.

You think you've got something nearly perfect, such as a good ending. Others who read your ending say (we hope politely) that it doesn't work. Whenever there is a conflict between something you like but other people don't, seek a consensus. If six people read your script and five of them love the ending, you're probably safe. If five of them note that your ending seems weak or contrived, you need to reconsider and probably rewrite.

Yes. I know. It's tempting to believe, "I'm the artist here! It's my work!" In fact, some people think being an artist is a socially acceptable excuse to become a maverick—to do as they see fit, answering to no one. That may work for novelists and poets. But I repeat—for the umpteenth time . . .

Drama is a *collaborative* art. First and foremost, your goal is to reach an audience. You accomplish that goal through your interpretive artists—that is, actors and directors. They will present your work. Therefore, you will always need their feedback and input. If you ignore the audience and/or your interpretive artists, you shoot yourself in the foot.

Lou Grantt was my first screenwriting teacher. (Yes, that really is *her* name, and no, she looks nothing like Edward Asner.) The former owner/publisher of *Hollywood Scriptwriter,* Lou started her career as a script consultant who had a special gift for working with novice writers.

I met Lou "back when." We were both struggling to get a foot in the Tinsel Town door. But as a film school grad, a former producer, and one of Linda Seger's protégées, Lou was light-years ahead of me. Not only did she teach me screenwriting, but she also taught me about the film industry. It was not an easy task.

I came to screenwriting from two decades of writing for print, plus producing and directing a lot of shows in non-profit theater, including three that I had written. I had a big ego, strong (albeit wrong) opinions, and no clue what I was walking into. At first, I argued with everything Lou said. (Ironically, many of my students do the same, leaving me to ponder the old saw, "What goes around comes around.")

Many of our early encounters were moments of truth that I had trouble facing. One in particular stands out. During a phone call, she explained that the kind of writing I do for print—yes, narrative prose—simply doesn't belong in a screenplay. I protested, as most beginners will, "Lou, this is my story. I can do what I wish."

Unruffled, Lou replied, "If you write for no one but yourself, yes, you can do whatever you wish. But if you want a career as a screenwriter, you will learn what film industry people want, and you will give it to them. Otherwise no one in the business will work with you."

Well, that hurt. But I didn't cave in. Like a spoiled brat, I continued to bang my head against walls. This included one episode during which I flexed my artistic muscles with a producer and blew my chances for a movie deal. That's when I began to see that Lou is right. The writer is only one cog in a big, complex wheel.

How do we handle the collaborative nature of our work? Kiss up? Throw our vision out the window? No, of course not! But by all means, chose your battles carefully. Resist only when it really matters. If the director wants a wink instead of a grimace, that's no big deal. But if he wants to throw out half the story and start over, you may need to take a stand (and risk losing the deal).

Yes, some people will cut your work to pieces simply because they have different tastes. They will want rewrites, not for the good of the script, but just to please their egos. You will recognize these people early on. Their tone and their terms are a dead give-away (such as lots of work for no money and not even the promise of a contract when you finish). You can choose to listen, but you don't have to do their bidding. (Such people can have good ideas, so I hear them out. Like chicken soup, it might not help, but it can't hurt.)

On the other hand, if a consensus among several readers indicates your script has poor structure or suffers from flawed logic, you have a problem. You might as well face it.

Yes, rewrite can be a struggle. You look at the baby that you have nurtured, and you feel like you are betraying the poor thing. Being an ostrich is the kiss of death, however, so approach your errors honestly and correct them.

Just remember: Becoming a dramatist is not a selfish process. It is not about following only your tastes and your interests, nor is it simply about being right. It's about using your talents to do the best possible job *for your audience.* To that end, bear in mind:

Nothing grows in a vacuum.

90% of writing is rewrite.

Kicking your ego out the door gives you more room to work.

EXERCISE 5

1. Prepare a "laundry list" analysis of three films you have seen but that you have not reviewed for these exercises. Write a commentary on each ending. How did the film . . .

    a. Solve the problem of the play?

    b. Complete its primary theme and play out its relationships?

    c. Provide a logical ending that satisfies the audience?

    (*Note:* If the ending did not accomplish the above, figure out why.)

2. Prepare a commentary of the ending for your screenplay. How does it . . .

    a. Solve the problem of the play?

    b. Complete its primary theme and play out its relationships?

    c. Provide a logical ending that will satisfy the audience?

3. Finish your script! Of course!

Chapter **Opening Doors**

You will hear it over and over. Writing a script is easy. Selling one is the hard part.

Now you have learned about preparing a screenplay that will work as drama and that is the crucial step. (Before you can sell a script, you must write one.) But until you have a high-quality script to offer, don't worry about agents or producers. (Most of my classroom students ask how to get an agent before they write Act One!)

Certainly, now you can read more complex "how-to" manuals about screenwriting and understand what the authors are saying. Many fine books offer additional information and ideas to help you complete your project. When at last you have a script ready for submission, you will come to the really tough part of screenwriting—marketing your material. I won't spend a lot of time on the subject. Far more qualified people have already written detailed volumes about it. But there are a few points I'd like to make.

Screenwriters face a maze of film industry circumstances they often don't understand. Paul Small was an agent for 15 years. He says, "The way we would like the business to work is not the way it operates. Going in, beginning writers have to realize that it is a complete business. It is said so often that show business is two words—and 'show' is a very small part of it. It is truly a business. Extraordinarily difficult." Small has always told actors and writers, "Unless you *have* to do this, do *not* do it." He thinks the only reason people should put themselves through the show business mill is because they have a passion for the work.

Every writer faces the grim prospect of finding representation and selling material. Even the most artistically committed may shudder at the task. Are there guidelines that can make it easier? Are there specific pitfalls to avoid? Talking with industry professionals who work in various venues, I asked, "What attracts you? What aspects are most likely to turn them off?" Without exception, they want *professionalism.* I repeat, nobody—but nobody—wants to work with amateurs.

More accurately, nobody has the time to work with amateurs. Agents and producers, after all, do not exist to educate writers. They are in the business of selling scripts and getting films made. Anything that impedes those goals wastes their time and time is money. Therefore, the screenwriters they choose must demonstrate professionalism.

PROFESSIONAL QUALITY

In nonprofit theater, I worked with actors who never earned a dime on stage, yet many had professional quality. One of my performer friends said, "Just because I'm an amateur doesn't mean I have to act like one." The same applies to writers. A professional will project competence, confidence, and style. Not anxiety. Not fear. Not doubt. (Underneath, perhaps they are quaking, but on the surface, you never see 'em sweat.)

Adopt the Boy Scout code: *Be prepared.* Know what needs to be done and get yourself ready to do it.

Certainly, if you are trying to interest agents and producers, you should contact people who seek your specific type of material. A "good fit" is essential. Producers get scores of screenwriter queries, most of which they ignore. First, the queries make it obvious that the writers know nothing about film, and second, they propose a project the producers would never do. Submitting your science fiction script to an agent or producer who handles TV comedies makes the individual wonder why you wasted your postage and his or her time.

Peter Duchow, whose 40-year history includes being an agent and an award-winning producer as well as a screenwriter, says to learn as much as possible about the people with whom you deal, then approach them appropriately. Paul Small specifies examining the Writers Guild of America (WGA) list and Hollywood Creative Directory to target the most appropriate markets. Roger Baerwolf at ShadowCatcher Entertainment points out that personnel turnover is brisk in film, and after a rejection, eventually it may be possible to approach the same company again. But, of course, second attempts work only when a writer follows the company trends and knows its current needs.

Obviously, if you are going to write films, you must learn something about making films. As a teacher, I repeat this constantly to my students. In particular, I explain they need to get behind a camera—*any* camera—and try to understand its effect on story presentation. Naturally, if you're going to be a doctor or a dentist, you study medicine or dentistry. Likewise, those who hope to succeed as screenwriters must study film.

Although formal training is not required for success, Paul Small mentions education as a visible benchmark of commitment on a screenwriter's resume. Attending a seminar won't say much one way or another. But writers who care enough to spend money and time in school making a formal study of their craft are firmly declaring their intention to be professionals.

BODY OF WORK

Build a writer's portfolio. Your scripts are your samples, proving you can deliver complete screenplays. Do you blanch at spending months writing something you may never sell? Me, too. As one who regularly writes for print and gets a check as a valid return for completed assignments, I find the "no-pay" situation in screenwriting hard to swallow. Yet, it's the nature of the beast because funding films is extremely difficult, and production is rare.

Indeed, payment on a screenplay can never be the only validation of its quality. Ironically, your best work may rate huge praise but earn nothing, even for an option. Roger Baerwolf notes, "Projects I loved have dragged on for years and finally fell by the wayside. It's heartbreaking, but that's the business." In other words, money aside, your only hope may be to write more scripts.

Paul Small recommends you have three or four screenplays ready, saying, "You have to look at an agent as a really well-dressed Fuller Brush salesman. You, as the writer, are one of his many brushes. If he can't sell you to his buyer—if you have only one look—you're going to be in trouble." If one "brush" doesn't attract attention, another might, so a writer needs a lot of material to offer.

"Writers write," Small concludes, "whether they're getting paid for it or not, because they *have* to write." In a similar vein, Baerwolf adds, "For heaven's sake, don't do it for the money. Do a script because you can't think of *not* doing it." Likewise, Duchow talks about "a fire in the belly," a passion and commitment so great that it cannot—and will not—be denied.

PROPER PRESENTATION

The entire first lesson in Chapter 1 explained that your script must be accurately formatted, properly punctuated, and free of typos and spelling errors. Every film industry person I have interviewed puts this requirement first on his or her list. Yet, over and over, I hear that 90 percent of the scripts they receive are improperly prepared. Considering the stakes, I shudder to think that any writer would risk so much over an aspect that is fairly easy to learn. With study and practice, this particular problem need not and should not exist.

In the same vein, you must learn how to *pitch* your script, especially on the phone, so that you will be ready when you are asked. When I was chosen a Nicholl Fellowship semifinalist, a prominent producer phoned, saying, "Pitch me your script. If I like the idea, I'll take a look at it." I had never pitched. Trembling, I muttered that my agent handled those things. He said he would call her. But he never did. I'm sure he figured if I couldn't handle a telephone pitch, I wasn't ready for the lofty atmosphere wherein he reigned.

Frankly, pitching terrifies me, but my only shot may be a one-minute phone call. So I know my material well. I have log lines ready. I check the trades to learn which venues my scripts might plug into. And I rehearse. All this helps overcome my fear.

Still, the task remains huge and daunting. With thousands of script proposals every year, agents and producers go to great lengths to set up meetings with money people. To protect their reputations and continue in the industry, they must offer the best material and writers they can find. With a professional attitude and well-crafted material, you give them, and yourself, an edge. So, if any secret combination will open Hollywood's doors for you, it is, quite simply:

"Think like a pro!"

Appendix

- Format Layout Grid

- Sample Script

↑TOP MARGIN - 1"   DIALOGUE COLUMN 3.25" WIDE (NO MORE THAN 3.5")   RIGHT MARGIN - 1"↓

```
INT. OFFICE - DAY

Chicago.  Columbus Day, 1919.  A leather upholstered
office. J. FILTHY RICH, a widgets entrepreneur, welcomes
REDNECK DOWDY, a beefy contract killer.

                    J. FILTHY
               (shaking hands)
          How do you do?

                    REDNECK
          I am delighted to meet you.
```

LEFT MARGIN 1.5 inches minimum from left edge of page

LEFT MARGIN 1.75 inches allowed

LEFT MARGIN 2 inch maximum

↑DIALOGUE Begins 3 inches from left edge of page.

↑PARENTHETICAL Indent 2.2 inches from left margin or 6 spaces from dialogue line. Confine to a 1.5 inch column..

↑CHARACTER NAME Indent 2.7 inches from left margin or 12 spaces from dialogue line. Type name in CAPS.

BOTTOM MARGIN - Can vary with length of dialogue, ranging from 1.5 inch maximum to .5 inch minimum. 1 inch is preferred, however. ALWAYS leave at least one half inch on the bottom margin.

<u>BRINGING IN THE SHEAVES</u>

An original screenplay

By Ira Goode Screenwriter

Ira Goode Screenwriter
13270 Madcap Boulevard
Sunnyville, OR 97372
Tel: (502)555-4532
Fax: (502)555-2345
Email: screenwriter@dash.com

BRINGING IN THE SHEAVES

FADE IN:

EXT. STREET - NIGHT

Monaco. Monte Carlo. A balmy blue evening.

A NUN and A PRIEST attired in traditional garments emerge from the Grand Casino. The Nun carries a satchel. Murmuring together, they amble to a side street.

A sleek white Ferrari waits in the shadows. The Priest opens the passenger side door.

INT. CAR - NIGHT

The Nun sits in the passenger seat, the satchel on the floor at her feet.

The Priest unlocks the driver's door and slides behind the wheel. Glancing at the Nun, he pushes his key into the ignition. Then, as if the gesture is foreplay, he reaches across her and fastens her seatbelt. She grabs him. Her mouth crushes his. He laughs.

                         PRIEST
              Darling! Wait!

                         NUN
              I can't. Winning money always
              turns me on.

                         PRIEST
              The casino people aren't fools.
              Suppose someone sees us . . .
              embracing?

                         NUN
              Oh . . . very well . . .

She releases him. He starts the car.

                         PRIEST
              But we're going back to the
              hotel. So just keep thinking
              those good thoughts.

EXT. HIGHWAY - NIGHT

A winding road. Below, churning surf. Headlights split the
darkness. TIRES SQUEALING, the Ferrari shaves curves.

INT. CAR - NIGHT

The Nun is buckled in. The Priest is not. She leans back
in her seat. He crouches at the wheel like a race driver.

                NUN
    I'm amazed we got away with it.

                PRIEST
    Oh, ye of little faith.

                NUN
    Funds for a new school?

                PRIEST
      (nods)
    In Zimbabwe.

                NUN
    Your babble about our poor
    little orphans. The suckers at
    the crap table ate it up.

                PRIEST
    And staked us nicely, too.

They laugh. Then, one eye on the road, he reaches into the
glove compartment. And brings out a .38 caliber automatic.

Her eyes fly open.

                NUN
    What are you doing?

                PRIEST
    Narrowing the odds.

EXT. ROAD - NIGHT

A GUNSHOT punctuates the SQUEAL of tires. Ahead the road
banks sharply. Missing the turn, the car hurtles into
space, noses over and plunges into the surf.

Bibliography, Recommended Readings, and Internet Sites

Bibliography

Ball, David. *Backwards and Forwards: A Technical Manual for Reading Plays.* Carbondale and Edwardsville: Southern Illinois University Press, 1983.

Hodge, Francis. *Play Directing: Analysis, Communication and Style.* Englewood Cliffs, NJ: Prentice-Hall, 1988.

Mamet, David. *On Directing Film.* New York: Penguin Books, 1991.

Moore, Sonia. *The Stanislavski System.* New York: Penguin Books, 1984.

Seger, Linda. *Making a Good Script Great.* Hollywood: Samuel French, 1994.

Recommended Readings

Egri, Lajos. *The Art of Dramatic Writing*
  Has chapters on film and plays. A classic that everyone should read.

Seger, Linda. *Making a Good Script Great* (Hollywood: Samuel French, 1994).
  This fine book on rewriting, structure, characterization, etc. is geared toward writers with some experience.

Seger, Linda. *Creating Unforgettable Characters*
  Invaluable in its in-depth examination of writing well-rounded characters.

Seger, Linda. *The Art of Adaptation: Turning Fact and Fiction into Film*
Deals with adapting plays and novels as well as real life events.

Trottier, David. *The Screenwriter's Bible*
A guide that is the closest to what is universally acceptable to nearly every agent and studio in town. For current order information, email dave@clearstream.com.

Whiteside, Rich. *The Screenwriter's Life: The Dream, the Job and the Reality*
Opportunities, jobs, markets, techniques, agents, producers, schools, and software.

Internet Sites

The Academy of Motion Picture Arts and Sciences (http://www.oscars.org)
A wealth of information about films and film history. For those who wonder what films to watch, the Academy site offers a webpage that lists every Best Picture winner since 1929. It also features a detailed section about the Nicholl Fellowship Awards, the undisputed queen of screenwriting competitions.

Drew's Script-o-rama (http://www.script-o-rama.com)
The best source for screenplays that have been produced.

Internet Movie Data Base (http://www.imdb.com)
Loaded with information about produced films and the people who made them.

Movie Bytes (http://www.moviebytes.com)
Lists *all* the screenwriting contests and competitions, as well as provides information on who's doing what deal with whom.

Word Play. (http://www.wordplayer.com)
From Terry Rossio who co-wrote *Shrek, Aladdin, Pirates of the Caribbean,* and *The Mask of Zorro*. Rossio's wise and witty columns about the craft and business of screenwriting are a mother lode that aspiring screenwriters should mine as soon as possible.

Writers Guild of America (http://www.wga.org)
This site is your inside track to the writer's side of show business. Here, you can peruse the WGA's standard contract or its signatory agents list.

Zoetrope Virtual Studio (http://www.zoetrope.com)

Francis Ford Coppola's gift to screenwriters, from first-timers to old-timers. An opportunity to read spec scripts in progress by writers working at many levels of development. A chance to ask questions that will help you learn how Hollywood conducts business. A place you can safely post your unproduced scripts and have other website members review them. (But be prepared to do some reviewing as well. You must read and review four scripts that other aspiring screenwriters have uploaded.)

About the Author

Originally trained as an actress, Wendy Jane Henson holds a bachelor's degree in theater arts and a master's degree in screenwriting. Working in educational and nonprofit theater, she produced and directed plays ranging from classical Greek and Shakespeare to Tennessee Williams and David Mamet.

Although she began writing for print when she was in high school, Wendy's early attempts at playwriting were "uneven." Writing and production of one-act plays led to a full length comedy/drama. A finalist in the American Playwright Program, the piece was produced in the Pacific Northwest. The next logical step seemed to be writing for film.

Wendy's first screenplay was a finalist in the Artist Trust Awards and then a quarterfinalist in the Nicholl Fellowships, sponsored by the Academy of Motion Picture Arts and Sciences. Subsequent scripts garnered awards and led to placement as a Nicholl Fellowship semi-finalist. Over the years, Wendy's material has been optioned, giving her experience with the stress and frustration of having scripts in development hell.

Since 1995, Wendy has taught screenwriting at Portland Community College, Portland State University, and Marylhurst University. She also served as a mentor for the Santa Fe Screenwriters Conference and taught online for the film industry trade magazine, *Hollywood Scriptwriter.*

Currently, Wendy lives in Portland, Oregon, with her family, who, she is amazed to find, remain remarkably tolerant of her passion for drama and writing.

Index